The Trilogy, Part Four.

Confusingly simple.

By Don Clampet.
(not my real name)
2021
Author of Tayto, Tea and Slimming World.
Author of Subway, Cycling and Shabbeycentre.
Author of Ambivalence is a Terrible Affliction

All royalties from all books will go to charity.
They will be split between:

Suicide Awareness & Mental Health charities.
Disability charities.

So, thank you in advance.

From the charities.

I just got in a row for pointing out that the London bridge terrorist was born and bred in Stoke, and one of the heroes who fought him repeatedly, and was stabbed repeatedly was born and bred in Poland.

I got called a snowflake, and told that people like me are part of the f@@@ing problem.

Ah well.
It's cold enough for snow.

2 Dec 2019, 17:15

I went to the shop for envelopes.
Only a couple of pence.
But I had no change.
So I handed her a £20.

She looked at me.
I looked at her.

Have you nothing a bit smaller, she asked?
I patted my pockets and shook my head sadly.

She looked at me.
I looked her.

I can't change it, I have no change left, she said.
I shook my head sadly.

She looked at me.
I looked at her.

I will have to give you all pound coins, she said, I have no fivers.
You can't give me all pound coins, I replied sadly, I have no belt on.

And I put my hands in my pockets to show how the trousers were at risk.
She looked at me, and the saggy baggy trousers.
She came to a decision.

Will you pay me next time you are in, she asked?
She suddenly seemed nervous.
Guarded.
Concerned.
But sympathetic too.
I will says me.

That settled it.
She wrote it in the wee red book that she obviously keeps for credit and off I went.

But.

She didn't ask my name.
She wouldn't know my name.
So I have no idea what she wrote down.

Possibly something like 'poor sad culchie eejit with saggy, baggy trousers and no belt'
'1 packet of envelopes'

Ah well.
At least they will recognise me when I go back.

4 Dec 2019, 14:35

I left the Hells Bells into work.

She got into the car.
She asked me how I was feeling with my cold.

But before I could answer she started talking.
And talking.
And talking.
I managed to get a word in on occasion.
Then the phone rang.
Wee sister.
She stopped my story and started talking to wee sister.
I managed to get a word in on occasion.
5 minutes later wee sister had to go.
She immediately started my story at the spot she had left it 5 minutes earlier.
The phone rang.
Big son.
She stopped my story and started talking to big son.
I managed to get a word in on occasion.
2 minutes later big son had to go.
She immediately started my story at the spot she had left it 2 minutes earlier.
And then we arrived at her work.

And off she went.
And peace and tranquillity reigned once again

Anyway in the 40 minute trip at no point was there silence sufficient for me to answer her question.

So if you see her, please tell her I am grand, my cold is mostly gone, just a touch of a sore throat.

But still.

I enjoyed the wee spin to Belfast. And wee sister. And big son. And chatty wife.
And now I'm off to work for some peace and quiet, all that chatting has strained my already sore throat.

Morning all. Isn't life grand?

5 Dec 2019, 09:09

Belfast airport.
Two English lads in front.
Chatting.

One pointed to a pipe in the ceiling.

Look at that he says, scornfully.
Look at fackin that he says.
That's so fackin Irish he says.
I looked too.
A straight pipe had a bend in it for no apparent reason.
It turned left, then right, then right, then left, and continued on the exact same height and direction as it was previously.
His mate agreed.
They must have had fackin corner pieces left fackin over and thought they would just put a fackin bend in it, he says.

Now.
I'm not gonna have some fackin English lads dissing the fackin Irish workman.
So I interrupted.

It's a fackin high pressure pipe lads, says me.
You can't have a fackin pressure pipe running for that length

straight, says me, patronisingly.
Or if there is over pressure you will blow every fackin seal down the far end, says me, scornfully.
So you put a bend innit like that to dissipate the fackin pressure, says me, patronisingly again.
And I tutted at their fackin stupidity.
Stupid English fackers with their straight fackin pipes.

Only one problem.

I have no fackin idea if it is fackin true.
No fackin idea at all.
No fackin idea if you put a bend in a pipe to dissipate pressure.

But still.
Accuracy isn't important.
A pair of arrogant fackin Englishmen getting schooled by a culchie fackin Irishman is important.

Tut fackin tut.

6 Dec 2019, 18:51

Dad?
Yes son?
Is the spare room warm enough Dad?
It's ok son.
Do you want the electric blanket on Dad?

I was very impressed.
He was very proud.

You have an electric blanket son?
Even better than that Dad, I have a culchie electric blanket Dad,

come in and I will show you Dad.

So we did.

Big son had put the outlet vent from the tumble-drier in under the duvet.

I won't deny it, it's a proud father moment.

And the bed is toasty warm.

7 Dec 2019, 09:59

I parked at the dam, and got ready to go for a mucky walk.
A man strode up to me.
Wellies. Dogs. Red hair. Camouflage gear. Proper walking stick.

They are crap off road, he says.
Sorry, says me?

Then I got cross at myself, because we shouldn't start sentences with sorry, that starts a conversation in a negative position, and the other person in a positive position, and wee habits soon become big habits and lifestyle habits. Say pardon instead.

They are crap off road, he says.
What are, says me?
Your car, he says.
Sorry, do I know you says me?

Shite. Did it again. Bloody sorry. See what I mean? Wee habits become lifestyle habits.

No, I'm just saying your car is crap off road he confirmed.
I don't take it off road, says me.

Well then why do you drive an off roader, he demanded?
Because its big and roomy and comfortable and can bump up kerbs,
says me.
You would be better with a people carrier, he declared.
But I don't like people, says me.

He looked at me as if I was strange. I'm used to that look, but in this
case I thought it was slightly hypocritical given that he appeared to
fairly high on the strangometer himself.

You would be better with something like mine, half the price, he
says pointing at his car.
I looked at it.
I wasn't impressed.
I decided to be as direct as he was with me.
Even with a strange, camouflaged, red haired man in the middle of
nowhere, carrying a stick.

But then I would probably have to approach complete strangers in
car parks and tell them how cheap my car is, says me.

He wasn't amused.
Him and his dogs got into his cheap car, started it up in a cloud of
black smoke, and spun the wheels going out of the car park.

Some seriously strange people about these days.
And some mildly strange ones as well.
And me.
I'm in the mix there too.
I decided to forgo the walk.
Too much muck.
I'm a bit like my car.
I'm not that good at off roading either.

12 Dec 2019, 11:55

I fancied a Choc Ice, so I drove out the lane.
I saw all the lights on in the Community hall.
I thought oh oh, that looks a bit like Slimming World.

I continued on out.
I saw all the cars parked.
I thought oh crap, that looks very like Slimming world.

I came to the end of the lane.
I saw all the dodgy characters hanging about.
I thought OH FECK, SLIMMING WORLD ARE BACK!!!

Then I saw the Polling station sign.

And I thought Phew.
I can relax.
They won't torment me for years like Slimming World did.
They will be gone tomorrow.
Phew.

Maybe some crisps with the choc ice would be in order. And a Coke.
With two sugars.
Medicinal purposes only.
I've had a nasty shock.

Fecking Slimming World. They haven't gone away ye know.

12 Dec 2019, 19:52

Help me out here Nordies.
I'm confused.
The lad at the next booth has a sectarian tattoo.
And I'm genuinely confused as to whether it is a Republican Tattoo,

or a Loyalist Tattoo.
I am.

It features Bart Simpson.
Who I understand, like Cuchulainn, is a bit of a Republican and a
Loyalist icon.
Cheeky Bart is urinating on a flag, but you can only see his back,
because we are permitted to display urination on a beloved and
respected national symbol, but not allowed to see a cartoon winkie.
This is something that appears to be condoned and indeed
encouraged by both Loyalist and Republicans.
They have a lot in common, it's surprising they don't get along
better.

The flag is the Irish Tricolour.

This would seem to indicate that this particular halfwit is a Loyalist.
Ok?
All agreed?

But the Tricolour is also on fire.

So the halfwit may actually be a Republican doing all he can to save
the flag from burning.
Hmmmm?
Hence my confusion.

It used to be simple.

If the tats were green and orange, to avoid getting beaten up you
pretended that for two years you were Mitchell McLaughlins
bodyguard.
If the tats were Red and Blue, to avoid getting beaten up you
pretended that for two years you were Jeffrey Donaldsons life
partner.
But now I am confused.

It's all Barts fault.

Anyway, as usual, God bless the Queen and the Healy Raes.
Cover all bases.
I'm off to price a tattoo of her Madge in a Healy Rae hat.
Urinating on Bart Simpson.

That will confuse them.

Confused.com

16 Dec 2019, 13:56

So anyway.

I walked into the living room to the Hells Bells, resplendent and
proud in my new Xmas jumper. Woolly, Red, Santa, what's not to
like? I was looking good, I was feeling good, life was good.
I did the auld posing thing, sticking my bottom one way and then
the other, smiling then pouting. Nothing too tarty ye understand,
tasteful like.
And I waited for the Hells Bells to respond.
No need to ask what she thinks.
When you are married to a Nordie, you realise that fairly quickly.
You never need to ask what a Nordie thinks.
The words 'what do you think' are largely redundant.
You are fairly certain of getting told what the Nordies think,
whether you ask or not.

She looked me up and down.
And down and up.

Feck me, she says.
Red is really not your colour is it? she declared.

Now.

Those of you not familiar with Nordieism may think that comment has negative connotations.

But you would be wrong.

That comment actually means 'you look good in black big lad, and I still fancy ye'.

So I will take that.

I went in to see the wee daughter.

Also a Nordie.

Baby Bells.

And I did the pose thing again.

She burst out laughing.

Feck me Daddy she says.

Was Santa on the sunbeds she says?

I looked down at Santa. He did appear to be of a swarthy tone.

More Shaquille Claus than Santa Claus.

That's possibly why it was on sale.

In PoundStretchers.

Was he in About Face she cackled?

Was he on the auld Isle of Paradise Ultra Dark she roared?

Was Santa in Santa Ponsa she exploded?

And she stopped there.

But only because she couldn't actually speak anymore.

I left it there too.

It's been a good day.

The Hells Bells still fancies me, and I made the Baby Bells laugh uncontrollably.

But next year I might go for a black jumper with a bloody snowflake on it.

18 Dec 2019, 08:44

I was cross last night.
I was settling down for a quiet night with a nice cold pint of diluted blackcurrant and a good book, but I was disturbed by music really loud and really late.
It made me cross.

But I wasn't cross at them, I was cross at myself.

It's the last Saturday before Christmas, people have a right to go on the sesh.
Good on ye I say.
Fair play.

But here is the problem.
Here is what made me cross.

There are three halls within earshot.
And the sesh was in one of them.
There is the Slimming World Hall.
There is the Mad Cult Hall.
And there is the Orange Hall.

And I'm cross because last night I was out lasted, out partied, out fought, out thought and out seshed by either Slimming World people, Mad Cult people, or Orange Order people.

None of whom are exactly what would normally be considered as 'party people'.

That's why I'm cross.
At myself.
And deservedly so.

I've let the side down.
Sorry lads.

I was sitting at the kitchen table.
I just sneezed.
A big sneeze.
A big uncontrollable head hurting explosion of a sneeze.
The wife ignored me.
No reaction.

The dog sneezed.
The wife immediately stopped what she was doing.
Maxie she says?
Are ye all right Maxie she says?
Poor wee pup she says.
Did you have a big sneeze Maxie she says?
Good girl she says.
Good wee pup she says.
Come here and give me a hug wee Maxie she says.
A big Sneezy Weezy from Maxie Waxie she says.
Great wee pup she says.

Anyway.
We both survived.
Me, sitting alone at the kitchen table.
Maxie, lovingly surrounded by family and friends.
Gesundheit, and Happy Christmas lads.

I enjoyed Christmas, but it hasn't been quite the same since I learned the truth about Santa.

27 Dec 2019, 19:14

I don't care.

I don't care what colour you are.
I don't care what creed you are.
I don't care who your God is, or whether you have a God.
I don't care what nationality you are.
I don't care what crisps you prefer.
I don't care if you are a drinker, or a pioneer.
I don't care who you support.
I just don't care.

If you are reading this, you are on my friends list, and you are my friend.
The rest of it just doesn't matter.

So Happy New Year.
Friend.

31 Dec 2019, 19:34

Wee daughter came in.

Daddy she says.
Yes says me.
You will be very excited about our university projects this term daddy she says.
Why says me?

You will love them says she.
Why says me?
Well the first one is all about golf tourism she says.
Wow says me.
We were thinking you could do it for us she says.
I could says me.
You would get a first she says.
Maybe I would says me.
You could teach the course she says.

Aye, all right pet says me.
Don't go OTT says me.
What's the second one says me?

Terrorist tourism she says.

Jaysus.
I'm sorry I asked.
What are ye trying to say pet?
Daughter wouldn't last long in Castlereagh, would she?
Does she not know that snitches get stitches?
Touts out?
Ye may try your mother for that one pet.
I wouldn't know anything about that.

3 Jan 2020, 14:46

One of those days.

I got told off for calling Leo Varadkar the Taoiseach, apparently I
should have clarified my answer with 'The Irish Prime Minister'.
I laughed.
He didn't.

Then I got told off for clarifying that nice man Boris Johnson the British Prime Minister as 'The British Taoiseach'.
Three times I did that.
And I laughed harder.
He still didn't.

Finally I got told off for clarifying the Stormont Assembly as feckin gobshites.
But I wasn't actually laughing at that one.
He was scowling.

Ah well.
I've lost a friend and gained a stitch.
Laughter is a terrible affliction.
But we could do with more of it.

9 Jan 2020, 19:02

It's ok not to be ok.
It's OK to cancel an appointment.
It's OK to not answer a call.
It's OK to change your mind.
It's OK to have a duvet day.
It's OK to want to be alone.
It's OK to take a day off.
It's OK to do nothing.
It's Ok to just get through the day.
But don't quit.
It's not OK to quit.

It's also OK to stop judging yourself.
It's also OK to stop berating yourself.
It's also OK to stop comparing yourself.
It's also OK to stop nurturing negative behaviour.

It's also OK to just get through today.
It's OK to rest.
But don't quit.
It's not OK to quit.

Samaritans 116123. 24 hours a day, 7 days a week. They are there now. If you need them.

Lifeline 0808 808 8000. 24 hours a day. 7 days a week. They are there now. If you need them.

So are your family.
And your friends.
And lots of people.
And maybe, just maybe, a chat, a friendly ear and a little bit of advice will get you through this.

And honestly? What have you got to lose? Make the call lads.

Just remember.
Even on the hard days, the shite days, the desperate days, the hopeless days,
Better days are coming.

Make the call.

11 Jan 2020, 20:06
I'm watching Cold Feet.
Memories.

Its 1998 again.
I've a full head of luscious brown curly hair.
I'm in my baggy stonewashed Jean's, matched with cowboy boots and a leather jacket.

I look good.
Run DMC is on the alarm clock radio.
It sounds good.
My lowered Seat Toledo GTi 16v with big boot spoiler is sitting outside.
It looks good.
I've a six pack of Tennent's cans, premium lager, I'm trying to go up in the world.
I had a tea from a new coffee shop, somewhere called Starbucks. It was good. I hope it lasts.
I'm taking calls on my Nokia 5190, which can store up to 100 names and numbers, and still has room for 3 games!! Wow!!

I'm worried about catching a new disease that's going round, something called a millennium bug.
I'm thinking it's time to sort out the wood chip wallpaper and the polystyrene ceiling tiles. They are starting to date.
The Euro has been launched, it will never catch on.
A new tv channel playing just music has been launched, but it too will never catch on.
The weather channel has closed, tv won't be the same.

But I like Cold Feet.
And that Seat Toledo GTi 16v.

13 Jan 2020, 22:06

Man came to see me to give me a price for a job.

That will be 450, he says.
450, says me?
Aye 450, he says.
Bit more than I thought, says me.
Hmmm, he says.

He thought about it.

Who do you support, he says?
Who do I support, says me, quite surprised?
Aye, he says.
Liverpool, says me.

He thought about it.

425, he says.
425, says me?
Aye 425, he says.
Cos I support Liverpool, says me?
Aye, he says.

I thought about it.

Still a bit more than I reckoned, says me.

He thought about it.

Who do you support locally, he says.
No one really, says me.
Hmmm, he says.
But I do have a soft for the Crues, says me.

He thought about it. He started laughing.

450, he says.
450, says me?
Aye 450, he says.
Cos I like the Crues, says me?
Aye, he says.

I thought about it. I started laughing too.

You a Linfield man, I asked?
Aye, he says.
Thought so, says me.

And we had a grand laugh and we settled on 400, which is still more than I wanted to pay, but we both got a turn.
And this crazy stupid mixed up corner of the world still makes me laugh.
Most days.

Wonder how much he would have charged me if I had said Leinster Rugby or Fermanagh GAA?

15 Jan 2020, 22:25

I thought the wife was quiet last night.
She didn't say much.
In fact, she didn't say anything.
I was working quite late, then I was in bed first, and fell asleep immediately.
I thought maybe I had done something to annoy her.
That would be a fairly regular occurrence.
Me and the dog house are well acquainted.
Ah well.

I woke up this morning and there was no sign of her.
I thought she had been very quiet going to work.
Good.
Then I thought maybe she was still annoyed at me.
Bad.
I thought I must have been fairly daft this time.
Very bad.
Ah well.

She phoned me this evening.
She was on the way home.
She was going to see her ma.
She would be late home.
Sort myself out for dinner.
Normal occurrence.
Ah well.

Then she mentioned wakening wee daughter up this morning, and how she was hard to wake up.
I was surprised.
I asked why would she be wakening wee daughter?
She told me her and wee daughter were in Dublin last night.
I was surprised, but then I suddenly remembered them saying goodbye yesterday.
When they left for Dublin.
And I had been distracted.
Oh aye says me.
I remember now says me.
That's why you were quiet says me.
You weren't in a huff says me.
You weren't even here says me.
Phew says me.

Turns out I wasn't in the bad books.
Turns out I haven't been daft.
Turns out I'm not in the dog house.
Turns out I was just alone in the house
Turns out that it wasn't that nobody was talking to me, it was that there was nobody there to talk to me.

Of course, I may now be in the dog house.
For not listening. Or for posting this. Or for not realising she had been missing for 26 hours.
Ah well.

Its where I'm most comfortable.

Nite all.

Anyway.

Today is the day when the new year's resolutions get broken, the diet gets chucked out the window, and the wine bottle gets opened again.

So I thought I would share something.

Several years ago I told you about a man I used to work with, he had been an alcoholic, he had lived in the streets for years, he had some severe side effects from this, the most obvious ones being a painful limp and a lisp. He only stopped drinking when he found out his daughter had passed away, and they couldn't find him for her funeral. He eventually got dry, he eventually got a job, he eventually told me his story over cups of tea in many parts in a wee security hut. He always wanted a brand-new car, and he achieved that too. I will never forget sitting in his new car, me with tears in my eyes, him looking at me like I was a feckin eejit. It's only a Hyundai he kept saying. It's only a feckin Hyundai. Jaysus.

I hold this man in the highest possible respect.

Last year he lost his job, he just wasn't physically fit enough. The years had taken their toll, he was old before his time. I was very worried at this. He went for a spin on his motorbike. I asked where too. I expected him to say Donegal or Portrush. He went further. He went to the South of France. And stayed for months. And did the Camino. And worked part time. And came home when he was ready. Months and months later. And still dry.

I met him last week. He went to an AA convention and clicked with a lad who was motor biking round the world. So, he decided to go too for a bit. He bought or blagged an old bike, a jacket, gloves and a helmet there and then, and took off for months. They slept in hostels and campsites and ate in diners and blagged sandwiches. He gave his AA presentations, the other lad fixed a few bikes, and they made a few quid to keep them going. He came home when he was ready. He donated the bike, helmet and gloves, but kept the jacket.

I told him he was the richest person I know.

He is now planning an epic charity event to give something back. He wants me to get involved, and I will. I looked at him, and his scrawny, painfully twisted stance, his dishevelled clothes, his poor speech and thought this was a wonderful idea. It may be too difficult, or possibly impossible for him, but I reckon he will do it. Nothing has beaten him yet.

Life has given him feck all, but yet he feels he wants to give something back.

Morning all. Happy Monday.

20 Jan 2020, 09:17

Ahhh lads it was lovely.
Just lovely.

I was coming out of Dunmurry heading for Belfast, just at the Cop Shop but before Makro.
Know where I am?
Aye?

A wee woman was coming the opposite way, and trying to turn into a narrow drive. And she made a pig's ear of it. And she started to reverse. Back onto the main road. And crossed over both sides of the road.

The car in front of me stopped.

He didn't beep, he didn't yell, he didn't wind down his window, he just stopped.

I stopped behind him.

The farmer in the jeep with the livestock trailer coming the other way stopped too. He didn't beep, he didn't yell, he didn't wind down his window, he too just stopped.

The lad in front got out of his car, and crossed the road, and moved the blue bin to make the woman's drive a touch wider. He couldn't go anywhere, he might as well. The farmer got out of his jeep and did likewise on his side of the road. And they both guided the wee woman into her drive.

And we all waited, both sides of the road totally blocked, with a car and a jeep with a livestock trailer.

Nobody beeped.

Nobody yelled.

Nobody gesticulated.

We all just sat quietly and waited.

And I thought it was lovely.

Just lovely.

A wise man once told me that there are only 6 arseholes in the world, there seems to be more but that's only because they seem to get around a bit.

I reckon he could be right.

Evening all.

22 Jan 2020, 17:26

I was being a bollox.

I was driving about.
I came to a junction, I was turning right, I had to stop. There was no turning lane, but I was to the right of the single lane, leaving a little bit of room to my left. Not enough for a car, but maybe a bike.
I had to stop, there was nothing coming from my right, but a steady stream of traffic from my left.
I had to wait.
All good?
Scene set?
OK then.

A car came up behind me.
I saw in the mirror.
I had one of those 'she's not going to stop, she's not going to stop, SHES NOT GOING TO STOPPPPP' moments.
It stopped, close enough to trigger my parking sensors.
And not just the beep beep beep 'nearly there now big lad' parking sensors.
It triggered the BEEEEEPPPP sensors, which mean 'about to go bang here big lad'.
But the car stopped.
And I started breathing again.

Then the engine started screaming.
And the driver banged the wee car up the footpath.
Front wheel, bang.
Back wheel bang, bang. It took two attempts to get the back wheel up. It was a big kerb.
And the car appeared beside me, turning left.

Little Korean car.
Grand.
I'm not a car snob.

Hefty lady driving.
Grand.
I prefer hefty people.
It takes more calories to frown than to smile, I find that's why
skinny people are usually miserable, and miserable people are
usually skinny.
Not always.
But usually.

Sitting too close to the steering wheel.
Far too close.
Not grand.
I don't like that.
It doesn't inspire confidence.

And scowling.
Not grand.
I don't like people who scowl.
I like happy, I'm OK with gormless, I can cope with morose, but I
draw the line at scowling.
And this lady was scowling.
This lady was putting effort into her scowling.
And she was scowling at me.
Because she still couldn't see up the road past me.

She edged out.
She scowled.
She edged out further.
She scowled.
She looked at me.
She scowled.

So I decided to get involved.
I looked right, and saw that the road was completely clear.
She was perfectly OK to go.

But I shook my head no, and put my hand up in a don't go signal.
I was enjoying her company too much.
She stopped.

And there we waited.

Me checking the traffic coming from the left so I could go, still no gap.
Me checking the traffic coming from the right so she could go, and there was nothing in sight, but I didn't gave her any indication.
I kept shaking my head sympathetically.
Her scowling at me.
Me smiling sadly back.

The she got peckish.
And she went looking for a snack.
Up her nose.
I couldn't look, but I couldn't look away, as half her finger and two knuckles had disappeared.
She struck gold.
She found a big crispy one with a big long springy stringy tail.
Her hand was halfway to the rear view mirror before the string broke.
I had to look away, I was retching.

I have no idea what she did with it, but if she flicked it she had to have hit my car.
There was nowhere else for it to go.
But I didn't hear a ding, and I haven't checked the car.
I think I would have heard a ding.
Or even a clank.
It was a biggie.
But I'm still retching every time I think of the big springy mucus string, gently wibbling and wobbling between her nose and her finger.

There appeared a gap in the traffic from the left, and off I went.

I don't know if she wondered why no traffic had gone past from the right, and why the road was completely empty after I had moved.
I didn't wait to find out.

I can still see the booger.
An the tail.
It's my own fault.
I was being a bollox.
And I have suffered for it.
Rightfully so.
Sleep will be a long time coming tonight.

26 Jan 2020, 17:09

I was chatting to a lad who has struggled mentally.
He went away.
He took a break.
And he came back different.
Better.
Improved.

I asked him what was different.
He told me what he had learned.
And I liked the way he put it.

He told me he used to focus on what he hadn't.
What he couldn't.
What he didn't.
What he shouldn't.

What he wouldn't.
What he wasn't.
What he isn't.

Now he focuses on what he has.
What he can.
What he does.
What he should.
What he would.
What he was.
What he is.

He learned to treat every day like its Friday.

SO HAPPY FRIDAY, EVEN IF ITS ONLY THURSDAY.

#itsoknottofeelok

30 Jan 2020, 08:56

Corrie finished.
Cold Feet was coming on.
I decided I wanted tea and toast.
HB decided to tidy up, while I was untidying down.
This was going to be tense.

She wasn't happy because I took a plate from the pile she was taking out of the dishwasher and putting away, so she put some more milk in my hot and strong tea.

I wasn't happy she had sabotaged my tea, so I messily took a knife and a spoon out of the drawer, just after she had put them all away.

She wasn't happy about the knife and the spoon so she barged into me lovingly and sent me flying across the room.

I wasn't happy about the barge so I put her wine glass back in the cupboard.

She wasn't happy about the wine glass, but then we heard the opening credits of Cold Feet so we called a truce and settled down to watch it.

I thought I had won, and was smiling away to myself on the basis that I had annoyed her three times and she had only annoyed me twice.

Then I tasted the tea.

And you know the worst?

I had to sit, say nothing and drink it all, rather than give her the satisfaction and concede it was rotten and make a new cup.
I blame Jimmy Nesbitt.
Him and his bloody Cold Feet.

4 Feb 2020, 18:18

I was in Dublin airport yesterday people watching.

The country kids were gas.
All excited.
Look mam, an aeroplane!!
Look mam, a jet aeroplane!!
Look mam, a jet aeroplane with and engine in the tail!!!
The townie kids sat watching, not reacting, smiling patronisingly.

And then a tractor went past.

Massey Ferguson.
4wd.
Nice yoke.
And the roles were reversed.

The townie kids got all excited.
Jaysus mammy, there's a feckin tractor at the airport!!
Look mammy!!
Look!!
The country kids sat watching, smiling away patronisingly.

Isn't life grand?
When little things amaze and amuse us?

9 Feb 2020, 15:10

My slight reticence against an Irish language act has been communicated in a fairly flippant and concise manner, by pointing out that the Irish for accountant is Cuntasoir, and I would prefer not to describe myself as a Cuntasoir.

I have received a reply, broadly in favour of an Irish Language Act, in a similar flippant and concise manner, pointing out that the Irish for a tiresome, annoying loudmouth is Trumpadoir, and it would be wonderful to describe such a person as a Trumpadoir.

Touche. As they say in Ireland.

10 Feb 2020, 17:45

I like Philip Schofield. He seems to be a good guy, and he gladly posed for photographs with my daughter and many others in an airport. I send him all my admiration and respect. I however am disappointed that in 2020 we still feel the need to discuss and publicise someone's sexuality, and require people to 'come out'.

However, in the spirit of unburdening and sharing, I too have something to announce.

Below my statement in full, which I have unashamedly copied

"You never know what's going on in someone's seemingly perfect life, what issues they are struggling with, or the state of their wellbeing — and so you won't know what has been consuming me for the last few years.

With the strength and support of my wife and my children, I have been coming to terms with the fact that I am grey.

My inner conflict contrasts with an outside world that has changed so very much for the better. Today, quite rightly, being grey is a reason to celebrate and be proud.

Please be kind, especially to my family, to other grey people, Desert Orchid, grey wolves and badgers.

Don"

11 Feb 2020, 10:41

A big lad.
A big lad who struggles with simple things that we take for granted.
A big lad who has hundreds of friends, and not a single enemy.
In that way, he has beaten every single person reading this.
Every single one of us.
We all have at least one enemy.

A decent, likeable, lovable gentle, big lad.

He wanted a breast of chicken.
Or a chicken fillet.
Maybe he couldn't say breast.
Maybe breast is hard to say when your speech isn't great.
Maybe fillet is a complicated word for him to learn.

So he asked for chicken.
Chicken with no legs.

And he made this cynical aul fella grin with pride and delight.

Chicken with no legs.

Nite all.
May you find someone who makes you grin with pride and delight too.

12 Feb 2020, 21:51

Its ten to nine.
I'm in my bed.
I've been here for 20 minutes.
And I don't care what anyone else thinks about that.

You see, some of you think its tiring reading stuff about me.
And others may think it's exhausting listening to me.
But have any of you ever considered how totally and completely draining it is BEING me?

So nite nite.
I'm logging out of Facebook.
I'm turning off the phone.

Unplugging the landline.
Closing the window.
Turning off the security cameras.
And I'm off to sleep.

See you tomorrow.
We ride at dawn.

13 Feb 2020, 20:56

Mental Health.

Start.
Start in a small way.
Start with a baby step.
Fix one thing.
Fix it right.
Seek improvement, not perfection, not yet.
And say WELL DONE ME!!!

Allow yourself positive thoughts.
Don't berate yourself for not finishing.
Never ever berate yourself for going slow.
Never ever berate yourself for taking a long time.
Congratulate yourself for starting.
WELL DONE ME!!!

Move on from what went wrong.
We can remember every bad thing, every insult, every negative
comment, every failure we've ever suffered.
Automatically.
But we have to focus, really focus, to remember the successes, the
compliments, the achievements.
WHY???

Why can't we say WELL DONE ME???

Focus on positive.
Remember things that have gone right.
Don't hide your scars.
Don't be ashamed of your scars.
Scars show essence, and experience.
Scars are earned.
Wear them with pride.

Find a way to surround yourself with creative people.
Or intelligent people.
Or caring people.
Or positive people.
Laugh.
Laugh long and loud and unabashed.
Drive with the windows open and blow the crap clean out of your
mind.
High five.
Hug.
Smile at people.
Wear a nice hat.
Fight for other people.
Fight for what you believe in.
Speak out.
Try new things, clear out clutter, go to bed early, wake up early.
Watch the sun rise.
Watch the sun set.
Let yourself shine.
And say WELL DONE ME!!!

Give other people a boost.
Promoting them inspires you too.
Demoting them hurts you too.
Criticism is too rampant, encouragement too rare.
The people dragging you down are always below you.

People lifting you up are always above you.
So try lifting people up.
A kind word.
A pat on the back.
Good work.
Thanks for that.
Good job.
Super.
Fair play.
Stop looking for perfect, but look for better.
And say WELL DONE ME!!

Fix yourself.
Your body can do anything, if only you could convince your mind.
A huge mountain won't stop you.
A tiny stone in your shoe will.
Get rid of the stone.
And say WELL DONE ME!!

Stop being afraid of what can go wrong.
Think of what can go right.
One positive thought can change your whole day.
One positive day can change your whole week.
One positive week can change your whole year.
SO START WITH THE ONE POSITIVE THOUGHT.
Say WELL DONE ME!!!!

Stop competing with other people.
Compete with yourself.
Your ego.
Your diet.
Your lack of exercise.
Your negative behaviour.
Your fears.
Compete with those.
Make yourself better.

You won't make yourself perfect, but you will make yourself better.
And say WELL DONE ME!!!

We all have made mistakes.
We all are making mistakes.
We all will make mistakes in future.
That's a given.
Apologise if need be.
Learn from them.
Move on.
You care much, much more about your mistakes than other people do.
Mistakes are bruises.
Anxiety is a bruise.
Depression is a bruise.
Bruises fade and disappear.
So do mistakes.

Do a bucket list.
Somethings you would love to achieve.
Make them huge and scary and almost impossible.
If it's not scary, then it's not big enough.
Then somethings that are achievable.
Set a specific target, in a specific time.
THEN DO ONE OF THEM!!!!!!
And then say WELL DONE ME!!!!

And ask for help.
It's OK not to feel OK.
It's absolutely ok to ask for help.
WELL DONE YOU!!!!

15 Feb 2020, 10:26

Lovely wee moment.
Maybe it translates.
Maybe it doesn't.
Maybe my description is bad.
Maybe description is impossible.
Maybe you had to be there
Maybe I have to tell you about the wallpaper, the old fashioned
dresser that every granny had, the big backed TV, the video tapes
piled neatly underneath, the Sacred Heart with the red light, the
pull out table that hadn't been pulled out in years, the mismatched
chairs, the saggy comfy seats in the corner, the framed photographs
yellowing with age, the big coal range with the twirly air vent, and
the brand new seldom used dishwasher, an obvious present.
Or maybe you can picture it.

Anyway.
I was visiting clients.
I go to them, I don't ask them to come to me, traffic is difficult for
them.
They are in their 70s, they live up the country, out in the country,
their family is nearby, and one son in his 50s lives with them.
Their son is a little bit too innocent for the world, or maybe the
world is a little bit too difficult for the son.
But they all get by.

We were sitting having strong tea in mismatched mugs and
homemade fruit loaf with lashings of butter on vintage plates with
heavy solid cutlery and chatting and gossiping about the price of
land and cattle and doing tax stuff, the son was sitting at the fire
watching TV.
A nice time was being had by all.
Myself included.

Dad, the son called over from the fireside.
Yes son, came the reply.
Am I warm yet Dad, the son asked?

Dad went over, and using the back of his hand felt his sons cheek, and then his tummy.

Not just yet son, he replied.
Five more minutes, he decided.
Thanks Dad the son said.

And Dad sat back down at the table with us.

And I just thought it was the most wonderful display of gentle family devotion I had seen in a long time.

Afternoon all.
I hope it translates.
Isn't life grand?

21 Feb 2020, 15:44

I like Cornettos.
So I went to the garage and I bought a multi pack of Cornettos.
HB likes Magnums.
So when I was there, I bought a multi pack of Magnums.

But.
I have just noticed something.
There are 4 Cornettos in the Cornetto multi pack.
There are only 3 Magnums in the Magnum multi pack.

Tomorrow night could be awkward.

Just one CornettoOoOo.........

23 Feb 2020, 19:24

Top road garage.
I got done.
Outsmarted, outwitted, outeverythinged.

And I enjoyed it.

I went to the butchers for the meat, then the shop for the bits and pieces for dinner, then went and paid and put them in the car.
Nothing out of the ordinary there.
Then I went back in to grab a subway.
Sweet chilli chicken salad, no jalapenos, cheese please, drop more sauce, and a diet Pepsi please, now ye have it, thanks.
Nothing out of the ordinary there.

And I left.

At the door there is a wee counter for giving out samples of the latest fare from the Eurospar range.
They do be tasty.
I spend 20 mins there one day last week.
I met loads of people I knew, and I shared some chowder with most of them.
And today my wee mate was working there and serving free samples chicken and broccoli bake.
So I asked for a taste.

No, she replied.
No, says me?
No, she replied.
Why, says me?
You have already bought your dinner, she replied.

This was true.
I had.
She had seen me.

She had served me.
3 minutes earlier.

And says me?
She put on her BT9 voice.
This is for prospective customers of chicken and broccoli bake, and
you are not a prospective customer of chicken and broccoli bake
and therefore you don't get any, she declared.
And she laughed in her BT38 way.
And laughed.
And laughed.
And so did I.
I laughed too.
She was funny.
And then she sighed and stopped laughing.
And so did I.

But she still wouldn't give me any free samples of chicken and
broccoli bake.

Outthought.
Outfought.
Outwitted.
But enjoyed the craic.

Lasagne samples tomorrow.
I like lasagne.
I'm going to bring my own cutlery.........

24 Feb 2020, 17:41

Potential new client.
Seemed to be always in a rush.
Seemed to be one of those people who require the world to bend

to their will, rather than the other way around.
Seemed to have a knack of finding obstacles, but avoiding blame.
Seemed to be constantly at war.

I didn't like him.
He didn't like me.

He complained about the traffic, but in his own special way. He
didn't say the traffic was heavy. He did say the road is full of silly
little foreign cars, driven badly, by benefit scroungers who really
should be at work at this time of the day.
So I added 'and yourself'
He didn't take it well.

He wanted Kenyan tea.
He asked me do they not do Kenyan tea in Carrickfergus, I told him
no, but then they don't do Carrickfergus tea in Kenya either.
He didn't laugh.
I didn't intend him to.

He commented negatively about my place being hard to find.
He had a point, it is hard to find. That's the whole idea of it.
I sarcastically replied that he called it hard to find, I call it exclusive.

He critiqued my attire, and was of the opinion that I should be
suited and booted.
He had a point. I was scruffy.
I replied that most people wear suits to justify their claims of
prowess, I don't need to justify, I just get stuff done.

It wasn't going well.
He had his doubts. I had mine.

Then things went downhill.
That's true.
The small talk had been excruciating.

And then things went really downhill.

He needed to phone HMRC to get the information that I had already told him I needed.
He went through the automated system, and 20 minutes later finally got answered.
He hmmed and hahed and answered questions for 5 more minutes, then he snapped.

Look, he yelled down the phone.
Stop, he yelled.
Could you transfer me someone that can f@ckin speak properly, he yelled.
Yes I will f@ckin hold, he roared.
I've been f@ckin holding for f@ckin hours, he bawled.

He turned to me.
He put his hand over the mouthpiece.
F@ckin stammering idiot, he declared.
Why the f@ck do they hire idiots like that to work in a f@ckin HMRC, he moaned.

I asked him to hang up.
He did.
I asked him to gather his papers.
He did.
I informed him that it wasn't working out and asked him to leave.
He did, after complaining vehemently about my attitude and promising that he would make sure that I would never work in this town again.
I succumbed to his level.
I laughed at him and told him to pa pa pa pa pa p!ss off.

Ah well.

People like that used to annoy me.

They don't anymore.
People like that now make me appreciate nicer people. Like myself, hopefully. And yourselves, definitely. And everybody else halfway decent.

Morning all.
I'm off to work on my short game and my twerking, because apparently my career is over.
Much love to you and your foibles and your bingo wings, bellys, hangups, scars, screwups, blemishes, frailties, fetishes, failings, impediments and all.
Appreciate them.
They make you you, and me me.
And never, ever, let some jumped up, power mad, shoulder padded, half-witted ignoramus demean you. Or anyone you care about. Or anyone else.

26 Feb 2020, 09:50

Iceland for a break. We went to see the Northern Lights.

I saw all the Iceland lads, with their cute beards that look silly on me, and their quirky hats that look ridiculous on me, and their big 4x4 with the monster truck wheels, and their fur lined jackets and their chiselled features and the way they stride through snow drifts while we stumble and fumble and fall and they smile patronisingly at our feeble efforts, and our women folk look at them with desire, and at us with derision.

And I reckoned it was time to even the score.

So I marched past them, in their whimsical hats and fur lined coats, in the sub-zero temperatures knee high in snow, wearing just boots, trousers and a t-shirt.
Quintessential mad Irishman mode.

And their women folk looked at me with desire And the local lads didn't like it.
Not one bit.

So there you go Mr Iceland and Mr Superjeep.is
You may have beaten England in Football and stuck the bankers in jail.
But I'm Irish.
And you can stick your chiselled cheekbones up your hole.

1 Mar 2020, 08:00

I love this place.

We were up the glacier.
Miles and miles of nothing, a road 100 yards away and 40 feet below buried under ice, maybe will reappear in 10 years, maybe never.
Completely empty.
Except one sign.
Which had been hit.
I expressed surprise that someone would crash into a sign when there was complete openness for a mile either side.
The driver just shrugged.
Maybe, he said.
Or maybe they just didn't like where someone put the sign he said.

And do you know something?
I agreed with him.
It was just the wrong place for a sign.

I love this place.
Fire and ice and happy friendly funny cheery people.

I'm self-isolating.
Just me. Bacon. Bread. Ketchup. And Tea.

Nothing to do with Coronavirus.

I've just had a run of cute townies who fall for every scam going,
and a run of cute culchies who miss every opportunity going.

See you all tomorrow, when I expect to be fully cured.

My 9am appointment didn't show.
Unusual.
No sign at 9.10.
No sign at 9.15.
Very unusual.
I got a text at 9.30, he had been delayed, he would be there shortly.
I was a touch miffed.

My 10am arrived.
My 10am left at 10.20, still no sign of my 9am.

My 9am eventually arrived at 10.30.
He apologised.
He had left the kids to school, as normal.
He had called in to see his Mummy, as normal.
She wasn't in good form.
She was worried about Coronavirus.
So he stuck the kettle on and stayed with her for an hour.

He expected me to be cross.
He expected me to be ratty.
He expected me to be busy, and to need to reschedule.

I wasn't.
I couldn't be.
We could squeeze him in.
A worried Mummy is more important than any appointment any day of the week.
In my book.

Anyway its Friday.
His Mummy is happier now.
He is good.
I am good.
Hope you are good too.
And your Mummy.
That goes without saying.

6 Mar 2020, 13:51

I was at a business breakfast meeting at the Asher's café.
A serious intense professional business meeting.
Until a glamorous granny with grandson walked in and sat down beside us.
Then business went out the window.

Firstly it's a bright day.
Bright sunshine.
Low sun.
Shining straight in the window.
And granny is wearing a fairly light flowery skirt and top.
And she is standing in front of the windows.
With the bright light streaming in behind her.

And she looks GOOD.
Completely clueless, almost naked, but GOOD.

And I take a fit of the giggles.
Childish but unstoppable.
But luckily so does the client.
Professionalism has gone out the window.

Granny is checking the menu.
We are regaining our composure.
Granny likes the look of the GF breakfast.
Gluten Free.
Scrambled eggs, bacon, tomato, and either hash browns or toast.
Which happens to be what I'm just finishing.
So granny decides to order the GF breakfast.

And the waiter comes over to take her order.
As I put the last tomato from my plate in my mouth.
And Granny asks for the God Free Breakfast.

And I explode.
Tomato all over the place.
Tears streaming down my face.
Snot spewing down my chin.
Tomato juice all over the shirt.
And the client is worse.

I try to turn it into a cough, but fail miserably.
He tries to pretend he is choking, but to no avail.
Everyone else is laughing too.
Maybe at us, maybe at granny.
We have to leave.
Neither of us is fit for anything.
Neither of us can trust ourselves to speak.
The staff appear worried.
Two big lads covered in tomato and crying and shaking and

sneezing.
I would be worried too.

He pays for ours.
I pay for granny's and grandsons.

Least I could do.

God free breakfast in Asher's.
Jaysus.
I love a granny.

10 Mar 2020, 12:38

The Hells Bells was going to see her ma.

So I told her straight.
I did.
I told her to be back here at 9pm.
The Hunted is on.
We like The Hunted.
Even though she calls it The Haunted.
But that's the Nordie accent.
Nordies can't say Hunted. They say Haunted.
Just like they can't say Terraced. They say Terrorist.
And also, they can't say Pouring. They say Porn.

But then I thought about it.

And I told her to be back here at 9.20pm.
So we could record the Hunted, and the Haunted, and play it back
and skip the ads but still finish on time.

I was all impressed with my boldness.

I felt powerful.
Empowered.
In charge.
Energised.
Envigored.

And then after she left I realised the Masters Golf is on.
Darn.
I like Golf.
Especially the Masters.
It's on until 10.55pm.

My boldness had muted somewhat.

Take your time pet.
No rush.
10.55pm is fine
Cup of tea.
Glass of wine.
Relax.
You do some pouring on the terraced area......

Ah well.
Even when I win, I lose....

12 Mar 2020, 20:50

The daughter got her ear pierced.
She got a wee blue heart, and every time she sees it she thinks of
her wee Daddy.
That's me.
Isn't that lovely?

While she was there the Hells Bells got her ear pierced too.

She just got a stud.

Nuff said.

I'm in Fermanagh.
I'm parked at a petrol station.

On one side of me is a Vauxhall Vivaro, with alloys, decals and chrome bull bars. The van is empty, the engine is running, and the door is wide open. Marty Mone is playing on the radio.

In the other side is an older scruffy Ford Focus. It too is running. Its driver has been cautious, in that he or she has closed the door. Maybe that's because he or she has left a baby in the back seat.

I'm parked in the middle, I haven't seen anyone move in at least 5 minutes, and I'm worried that if I turn off my car and lock it when I go into the petrol station, they will all laugh at me for my naivety.

Also I think I might be minding the baby.

I love Fermanagh.
Things like this only happen to me in Fermanagh.

Man to man.

A mate phoned me at 10am during the week.
U fancy brekkie he says?
Aye says me.

I'm just finishing a bit of work says me.
5 mins and then I will be down says me.
So I did.
Then I went.
He had the teas ready.
We knew what we wanted. The cafe knew too.
We ordered, we ate and sorted out business.
And I was back at my desk 45 mins later.

Man to woman.

The wife came in to see me.
U fancy brekkie she says?
Aye says me.
I'm just finishing a bit of work says me.
5 mins and then we will go says me.
And she waited.
And strummed.
And humped.
And sighed.
And strummed some more.
Strumming makes me slow down.
So does sighing.
The 5 mins took 10 mins.
Then we left.
She decided she had a soft wheel, so we had to check the tyres.
She then had to take the bin in, but we left it till we got back.
She then had to drop something to her mates house, but she was just dropping it off, and she definitely wasn't going in, because her mate was working.
She went in.
I waited.
We made the cafe, and we deliberated before ordering.
The waitress wasn't upset at the delay, she saw a wife and knew that it wouldn't be quick.
We ordered, we ate and we sorted out business.

On the way back I brought the bin in.
And I was back at my desk 90 minutes later.

14 Mar 2020, 16:49

Bit of a solution lads for the St Patrick's day cancellations.

St Declans day.
24th July.
Summer.
Warm.
Virus will be gone.
Schools off.
Self-isolation will be a thing of the past.
Think about it.

Also St Declan qualified for Ireland by birth, not like the plastic
Paddy who qualified under the slavery rule.
And St Declan is based on a beach in Waterford, St Patrick is on a
rock in Ballymena. Let's be honest lads, Ballymena isn't exactly
known for the sesh. The Paisleys, buses, sashes, nepotism and mad
churches, yes. Party and a sesh, no.
Waterford (the Deccies) (the gentle county) is the sunny south east,
beaches, amusements, Crystal, round towers, proper saints and a
good sesh.
It's a no brainer.

As for timing I think you will find that July is a grand month for an
auld parade, bit of music and a sesh, the protestants have been
doing it for 300 years. Time we had a go.

So there ye have it.
See you in July.
On the 24th.

Don't mistake it for the one on the 12th. That's a different celebration altogether.

UP THE DECCIES!!!!!

15 Mar 2020, 13:13

I'm a middle child. A Middleborn. I'm always excluded, ignored, marginalised.

I fully expect not even Coronavirus to put me first.

Here's to all the Middleborn. Our time has come.

Cheers

17 Mar 2020, 17:30

BRILLIANT NEWS!!!!

FINALLY!!!

ALL SLIMMING WORLD CLASSES HAVE BEEN CANCELLED!!!

INDEFINITELY!!!

And the world just got a little bit brighter.
Curry chips all round.
They are now Syn free.
And a coke.
With two sugars please.

18 Mar 2020, 21:58

I'm not particularly worried about getting this virus.
I'm big and strong and belligerent and fit enough to fight it.
Not even Coronavirus wants to take me out.
So I'm not particularly concerned about it.

I am however worried about giving the virus to someone who isn't
quite as big and strong and belligerent as me.
Someone who isn't quite fit enough to fight it.
I'm not worried about getting it.
I'm worried about spreading it.

And that's why I'm keeping my head down, changing a few habits,
and washing my feckin hands.

I don't think it's much to ask.
Morning all.
Sun is shining.
Isn't life grand?

20 Mar 2020, 08:13

Unforeseen result of Coronavirus epidemic.

Nordies are back talking about the seetuation again.

That's when you know it's not good.

23 Mar 2020, 15:34

I'm genuinely humbled.

The shit has hit the fan for the self-employed, for the employers, for the company directors, for the small business owners.
For the people I work with.
And everyone I work I consider friends.
Some are new friends, some old friends, some pain in the backside friends, but all are friends.
And I have had to try my best help them.

Last week I had the worst week ever in work in many years, I had to issue 107 P45s.
We managed to set up schemes to save hundreds of jobs, but 107 were lost, and businesses closed.
A lot of jobs lost were by people I know.
With families I know.
And people are hurting.

But.

Without exception,
whether we have managed to save jobs and businesses and livelihoods or not,
whether the news has been good or bad,
whether we have had a success or a failure, without exception,
the people involved have thanked me,
and sent their best wishes to me and my wee family,
and told me to take care.

That's why I'm humbled.

In the middle of madness, simple humanity shines through.

24 Mar 2020, 11:53

We have settled into a wee routine.

I'm making the breakfast; the Hells Bells is making the dinner.

It's currently a tight call as to whether Coronavirus or Food Poisoning gets to us first.

Morning all.

Isn't life still grand?

25 Mar 2020, 10:09

Big sons' mate has come to see him.

But they are self-isolating.

So his mate is sitting in the van. Window down. Chatting.

And big son is sitting in the car. Window down. Chatting.

And just to annoy them, I have ordered a Dominos.
Delivery.
Whose driver will blind them with headlights as he comes down the drive.
Park in front of them.
Then walk between them.
Carrying pizza boxes.
And I haven't ordered anything for them.
Just for me.

I've missed big son. I'm glad he is home.

25 Mar 2020, 20:12

Hells Bells is off today.
She is having a lie in.
I'm downstairs working.
I'm hungry.

I called up to see if she wanted breakfast.
She didn't answer.
I got worried.
She has had a cough.
She also has a sore leg.
What if she was sick?
What if she collapsed?
I hadn't heard from her in hours.
Now I'm scared.
I dashed up the stairs
I opened the door carefully.
The room was in darkness.
Hells Bells I panted.
No answer.
Hells Bells I panted, slightly louder.
A weak voice replied.
Yeah it groaned.
Thank goodness.
I was so relieved to hear her voice, even though the weakness in it
it broke my heart.
U ok pet says me?
Yeah she replied.

So brave.

You want some breakfast I asked?
No she replied plaintively.
You should eat something says me.
Maybe later she replied sadly.

So brave.

What about if I make breakfast and bring it up to you says me?
Aye, that would be nice she replied.

It brought tears to my eyes.
The poor, poor woman.
Going to try to eat just to please me.

So brave.

I made crispy bacon as she likes it.
I made scrambled eggs.
I made toast, crispy on the bottom, softer on the top, so she could choose whichever she was able to eat.
I put some ketchup on the plate in the shape of a wee heart, but I ballsed it up and it ended up looking like a turd.
I made the tea slightly milky to ease her sore throat.

So brave.

I carried it carefully into the room.
It was slightly brighter.
I could see her.
She had turned towards me.
Big sad eyes filled with tears.
I set the plate and the tea on the beside locker.
How are you pet says me.
She looked at me.

So brave.
So stoic.
So sad.

I'm watching Greys Anatomy she replied tearfully.
Doctor Alex has just left she says sadly.

For good she says, distraught.

That explains that then.
Nothing brave or stoic about it.
She was quiet not because she was ill or at deaths door, she was
quiet because she was watching Greys bloody Anatomy on the
kindle under the covers.
And getting me to make her breakfast in bed.

I hope she enjoys her ketchup turd.

27 Mar 2020, 11:53

Does anyone else think that maybe we as a society valued things
and we undervalued people, and that we may have been found
out? That maybe we are chasing the symbols of happiness instead
of happiness? Maybe we overvalued celebrities and sports stars,
and undervalued nurses, doctors, carers, farmers, production staff,
delivery staff? Maybe in future we won't be as obsessive with
people above us, and less dismissive of people below us.

Does anyone else think that maybe we won't expect people to be
there to serve us, and maybe we will thank them for being there to
help us? Maybe we won't dash to the doctor or A&E just as quickly?
Does anyone else think that maybe we got a wee bit gobshitey, a
wee bit wishy-washy, a wee bit objectionable, but we might not be
just as in future? Maybe we will stop getting so offended at things
that are of no consequence to us? Maybe we will stop judging, and
start listening?

Does anyone else think that we need to be a bit more independent,
and a bit less dependent?

Does anyone else think that maybe the green and orange shite won't be quite as important in future and that maybe people having homes, decent wages, and a quality of life is more important? Maybe we will stop inventing enemies, and start looking for friends? Maybe we will stop looking to exclude, and start looking to include? Maybe we will stop listening to people who shout the most, and start listening to people who speak the most sense?

Does anyone else think that we might be a little bit more grateful for what we have, and a little bit less concerned for what we don't? We might be less demanding, more accommodating? We might realise that the greater good beats personal inconvenience? We might realise that we need to treat the planet better, because like it or not, we are bolloxed without it?

Does anyone else think that maybe we will look at and address failures in ourselves as a society, rather than looking at and condemning failures in others?

Maybe we will be who we are, instead of being who we think we should be.

Is anyone else worried sick about family and friends, and hoping that things get back to normal soon? Maybe more normal, but not quite as we were? Maybe we will have improved? Does anyone else wish we could have done something like this without so many people suffering?

Stay at home.
Keep your head down.
Stay safe.

30 Mar 2020, 13:02

I was making breakfast.
I went to see the Hells Bells.
What do you want for breakfast says me?
Whatever you are making she says.
Poached eggs and toast says me?
Aye she says, gleefully.
And veggie roll says me?
She screwed her face up.
No veggie roll she says.
Ok says me.
Ok she says.
Ready in 10 says me.
Ok she says.

I got the veggie roll, 3 pieces left in the packet.
I decided to stick all 3 under the grill.
Feck it.
Live a little.
Life is too short.

The veggie roll bubbled away nicely.
I stuck on the eggs, and the toast, and turned the veggie roll and made the tea.
Things were looking good.

I earmarked one piece of veggie roll as my favourite.
It had a nice big lump of onion poking out.
It would be nice and crisp on the outside, warm and soft on the inside.
Yum yum.

The toast popped.
Yum.
I buttered it.
I called the Hells Bells.
I took the veggie roll off the grill and on to my plate.

Looking good.
Yum.
And I got the poached eggs, and gave herself the two nice soft runny ones, and me the ones that had burst and were stringy.
Yum for her.

She came in.
She sat down.
She looked at me.
I looked at her.
There was a pause.

Give us a bit of veggie roll she says.

I knew it was coming.

I gave her a bit.
Ah well.
No point getting upset.
Life is too short and all that.

She started to eat.
I started to eat.
She stuck her fork into the veggie roll.
And then I saw the bit of onion.
Crisp on the outside, soft on the inside, the piece I had earmarked for myself.

I told her to stop.
I lifted a dry scrawny end piece of veggie roll off my plate and popped it on hers, then I snagged the nice bit straight off her fork.
That's my bit says me.

She looked at me stunned.

Feck it.

Life's too short.
Buts it's not that bloody short.

Yum.
Morning all.
Isn't life grand?

31 Mar 2020, 11:23

I was reminded of a wonderful Ulster Scots expression this morning. Excuse the spelling, I'm not fluent.

It's no wha ye do or wha ye hey.
Its wha ye do wi wha ye hey.

2 Apr 2020, 11:43

It's all still there you know.
Nothing much has changed.
Not really.

When this is over, I'm going to Rosknowlagh, I'm going to go for a big walk along the beach, and round the corner towards Murvagh. I've never done it, I've often said I must do it, but I never have. And it's all still there.

And I'm gonna drag the Hells Bells with me, and I'm even gonna hold her hand for a wee bit and make her happy as we walk along the beach. She likes holding hands the odd time. The beach is all still there.

And then I'm gonna get caught out by the tide on the way back, and

I'm gonna climb over the rocks and sand dunes and back to the car, and I'm not gonna give a shite about any muck on my shoes or in the car. I might have to let go of the Hells Bells hand as we clamber, I'm sure she will understand. The sand dunes are all still there.

Then I'm gonna drive up to Smugglers, and I'm not gonna worry about parking even though it's always a disaster parking there. I bet you there are loads of spaces in the car park now, Smugglers is all still there.

And I'm gonna go in and ask for a table, and the big lad that works there is gonna say it's gonna be an hour, and I'm gonna be quite happy with that, and I'm gonna get a pint of their finest diluted orange for me and a Hendricks and slimline for her and we will sit in the bar and chat to everyone and become best friends for the next 45 minutes then hate the feckers when they get a table before us then become best friends again when we sit beside them. The bar is still there you know.

When I get the table I'm gonna order whatever I fancy at the time, while keeping the diluted orange and the Hendricks flowing as we sit watching the sun go down between Killybegs and Ballybodonnell and the Slieve League cliffs, and Mullaghmore and Mayo on the other side, they are all still there you know.

And then I'm going to go back to Fermanagh over the mountain road with a passing nod to the Gates of Hell at Lough Derg and a quick howaye to St Christopher to get me safely home. It's all still there you know.

We may be stuck here, but it's all still there.
The only thing that has changed is me.
I'm not going to take it for granted next time.

Evening all.
Stay safe.

See you soon.
Very soon.

Working from home together is wonderful.

My work habits have just been kindly critiqued and analysed, they are putting me at risk of back and neck pain, and I need to reconsider my methods.

I've been working from home for 20 odd years, she has been working from home for 2 weeks.

I bow to her superior expertise.

Morning all. Isn't life grand?

Socially distanced, local area walk.

It's easy to figure out someone's religion up here, Catholics walk on the left, Protestants walk on the right.
Don't know why.
Don't know how.
They just do.

Check it out for yourselves.

Ps. This is just an observation, not a judgment. Both sides are equally valid and have parity of esteem in my opinion. Don't complain to Nolan about me. Again.

Never thought I would see the day.

49 years of age.
Friday night.
Sitting in.
Watching television.
And missing me Mammy and me Daddy.

Stay safe lads.
See you all soon.

I'm watching a program called Greys Anatomy, via a dodgy link on modern technology, connected through a yoke called an Amazon Firestick, plugged into a spare room TV, with the Hells Bells beside me and her not talking.

This is all new to me.

Happy Easter.

Funny one isn't it?

Stuck at home.
Not seeing family and friends.
Bit crap isn't it?

Yes, it is.

Except.

You could always make the most of a bad lot.

You could do sit ups, push ups, squats, burpees, plank? Start with 10 of each, 30 seconds of plank. Takes a couple of minutes. Then repeat.

Start a journal. Or a blog. Or a book. Or a song. Or an album. Or poetry. Seriously. Right now, on your phone. I did. Thrice. And everyone I ever met has a story to tell. Everyone. So, tell it.

Make a list of people you have promised to catch up with but never have. And message them. Tell them. Don't feel guilty, phone lines go both ways. Then when this lifts you will be ready to go. And stop making excuses. You are brilliant at excuses, you can stop making them now.

Dig out the guitar, or banjo, or piano, or drums, or bodhran, or harmonica, or tin whistle. Music is brilliant. And free lessons are all on YouTube. And you have plenty of time now, right? Or are you still making excuses?

Run. Cycle. Walk. Climb a mountain. Slieve Donard is 200 flights of stairs high. Carrantuohill is 240 stories. Start with one flight now. Do it in your jammies and slippers.

Practice your Golf short game. Or your Football skills. Or your Hockey skills, GAA skills, Rugby skills. Maybe you can't practice your long game, but you can definitely work on your touch and control.

Bring the partner. If they won't join in, use them as a target.

Read a book. A big book. A long book. Settle down in the corner with a rug and a glass of wine and get seriously lost in a big book. No better place to get lost.

Cook. Why are you still making convenience foods, when you have time to make fresh foods? Or is that an excuse I hear?

Garden. I don't mean cut the grass. I mean properly garden. I mean plan it out, have a beer, think about it, have a gin, design it, have a glass of wine, and start the work when you sober up. Suns out, guns out.

Create a viral video. Make it fun. Something people might like to share. You have the phone, you have the camera, you have the Wi-Fi, you have the time. I have a great idea for one, I'm off to do it now.

Sort out the old photographs. And actually, look at each one. And share a wee memory and jot it on the back. It can be the place and the year, or it can be that time something amazing or funny happened. I prefer the amazing funny things. And smile as you do this.

Watch all the films that you were too cool to watch before. Or series on Netflix. Become a study in naffness.

Make a list of things you are going to do when this lockdown lifts. I'm going to do Benbulben and Croagh Patrick, Carrowkeel and Keshcorran caves. I'm off to Sligo and Mayo for a weekend. After I hit Rosknowlagh that is. All of you are welcome.

Look around you. But actually look and notice and see. You have time. Appreciate what's there. Take deep breaths. In through your nose, out through your mouth. Smile at people. Nod at people.

Speak to people. Acknowledge people. You might be the only people they will see for a while. Sleep in. Lie on. Rest yourself. Be ready. When this lockdown lifts we are all going to be busy.

But stop with the bloody excuses, OK?

Happy Easter.

12 Apr 2020, 11:42

It's a trap lads.
It's a great, big, dirty, girly trap and I walked straight into it.

I watched an episode of Greys Anatomy the other evening.
Just to keep her company.
It was on some Nutts Corner market hookey gadget, and we were being rebellious.
We were sticking it to the man.
Yeeeooooo.
Plus I was enjoying the silence.
These things happen in lockdown.

But it was a trap.

I watched Greys Anatomy.
Now apparently I have to watch Grey and her Anatomy from the start to get acclimatised.
Backup.
So I know what is happening and why the relationships are fraught with fragility and frailty.
Plus I have to watch Station 19 because it intertwines with Greys Anatomy.
And I have to watch Killing Eve because it stars someone who used to be in Greys Anatomy years ago, even though I haven't seen it,

but when I do see it I will recognise her, and my life will be fulfilled.

I thought there were 16 episodes of Greys Anatomy.
There aren't.
There are 16 series of Grey and her Anatomy.
And each series has like 24 episodes.
And she possibly falls in love in every single one.

Ah well.
That's a lot of anatomy.

On the plus side, that is also a lot of silence.

Anyway.
I'm done for lads.
Save yourselves.

See you when all this is over.
It's a beautiful day to save lives.

14 Apr 2020, 10:52

I will be honest.

I'm now missing the Mammy, the Daddy and the Barber.

14 Apr 2020, 19:53

The Hells Bells washed the floors yesterday afternoon.
She told me to stay off the floors.
She gave me the serious voice.
The Nordie voice.

The 'there won't be any messing, so there won't' voice.
The 'I'm not joking, so I'm not' voice.
So naturally I stayed off the floors.

Quick question?

Do you think they would be dry yet?
Would I be safe to walk on them?
I keep hearing that Nordie voice.
Do you think I would be safe?
Maybe give it another day?
Or a week?

Morning all.
From me, at the bottom of the stairs, scared to go any further.

15 Apr 2020, 11:34

Morning all.
We need to chat.
A serious chat.
So sit down a minute.
And read this please.
Just one minute.
Thanks.

Standards are dropping lads.
Too many of you are being a wee bit silly.
A wee bit gullible.
And you will suffer for it

See these Facebook competitions?
And others like it?
250 free unmarked TVs from Argos that can't be sold?

10 free holidays because the previous winners were all under 16?
10 huge RVs because the previous winners don't have driveways or driving licences?
Missing people with no place details or no dates?
Or a page that only has one post?
And the page was set up last night just before midnight?
But has been shared 40k times?

Here's how it works.

It's called Phishing.

They set up a page giving away a mad prize.
No names, no phone numbers, nothing.
They use fake Facebook profiles to like and share it thousands of times.
It comes to you.
You see it, you like it, you share it.
Thousands do it.
They now have your name, email address and phone number.
AND THEY KNOW YOU ARE GULLIBLE.

So now you will start getting text messages telling you that you are entitled to a rebate from O2, click on this link and enter your bank details. You aren't. It's a scam. But you told them you are gullible.

And you will get text messages that you are entitled to a rebate from HMRC, click on this link and enter your bank details. You aren't. It's a scam. But you told them you are gullible.

And you will get threatening calls that you owe Sky or BT or HMRC a few quid, and to stop legal action you need to pay NOW. You didn't, you don't, it's a scam, but you told them you were gullible.

And calls asking for help for a poor deformed child with a cleft palate and a club foot. There is no child. The child is a 48-year-old

Russian gangster who wants a penthouse in Monaco. And you told them you were kind, but gullible.

Or you might actually win the car, but you need to pay £200 to get it shipped. Hundreds of people will win it. None of them will get the car. But you told them you were gullible.

And dozens and dozens of little ways they will try to catch you out. All because you gave them your email and phone number and told them you are gullible.

AND THEN YOU COME TO ME.

And you tell me you have lost your £30k life savings when you thought you were getting £26.40 refund from O2. This is true. This has happened.

Or you tell me you have invested in parking spaces in a field fifteen miles from Glasgow Airport and are going to make an 80% return. This too has happened.

Or you are being persecuted by HMRC for debts and why the hell do you have debts when you pay everything promptly and what the hell am I doing about it? This happens monthly.

SO.

Please think before you share.
Just check it out.
Protect your future reputation.
And your bank balance.
If it's for a free fish supper from the local chippy or a fourball in Donegal, feel free. It's probably not run by Russian gangsters or Chinese Triads.
But if it's for a Range Rover, or an RV, or free holidays, or free TVs, on a page set up yesterday, no other posts, no contact details........

Don't tell them you are gullible.

And don't ever tag someone you like. Don't drag them into this too.

16 Apr 2020, 09:31

I went up to the butchers.
They were busy.
4 lads working.
As usual fairly jovial, fairly giddy, fairly chatty, fairly good form.

A wee man in front of me.
He was being a wee bit slow, a wee bit careful, a wee bit deliberate.
Sort of wee man who finds everyday life a wee bit of a struggle.
Harmless wee man, minding his own business, doing his best and getting by.

He asked the server for a handful of mince.

Now.
I know what a handful of mince is, it's a about a pound of mince, maybe a pound and a bit.
The wee man knows what a handful of mince is, it's enough to fit in your hand.
The server should know what a handful of mince is, you take your hand, you fill it with mince, you have a handful of mince.
It's not difficult.

But the server decided to laugh at the wee man.

He nudged his mate and asked the wee man if he wanted left handed or right handed mince and the two of them had a nice wee chuckle.

The wee man was confused.
And a touch upset.

I was next in the queue to order.
So I loudly asked for a handful of mince too.
And I stuck my chin out and glared at the servers, daring the two of them to laugh at me.

The giggling quickly stopped.

To be fair to the butchers, the boss stepped in. The wee man left happily with a wee parcel of meat on the house and his handful of mince, no apology because an apology may have caused further upset. The boss knew his stuff. I left with a handful of mince and an apology I didn't warrant or want but I accepted it on the wee man's behalf, and I reckon that two servers would have left with a fly in their ears and a boot in their holes. The boss knew his stuff.

So all in all it's been a good day.

Except I only went in for a few sausages for breakfast in the morning. And I've ended up with mince. A handful of mince. Ah well.

17 Apr 2020, 17:00

A few days ago.
I was sitting in the kitchen.
The Hells Bells walked in.

I'm just getting a drink of water she declared.

Nordies do a lot of declaring.
I don't really know why.

But they are all wild fond of a nice declaration.

Anyway.
I'm just getting a drink of water she declared.
She poured her glass of water.
I just waited.
Every time she pours water she needs to pee.
Women cannot pour a glass of water without needing to pee.
Gin yes, wine yes, water no.
I need to pee she declared.
And off she went.

I decided to have some fun.

So I filled her glass to the brim with diluted orange.
Right to the brim.
Just for the hell of it.
It's like an adventure sport.
Wind her up, and let her go, and then tell her to Calm down Arlene.

She came back.
She saw the glass.
F@ck sake Don she declared.
I smiled like an eejit.

She took a sip.
It was too strong.
F@CK SAKE DON she declared.
I smiled like an eejit.

Nearly there now.

She went to the sink to pour some out.
I just waited.
There was cutlery in the sink.
Women can't leave cutlery in the sink.

I knew she couldn't.
So she poured some orange out and put some water in and put it to the side to tidy up the sink.

And I drank the orange.
Then ran for it.

OH FOR F@CK SAKE YOU AGGRAVATING GOBSHITE she yelled.

But I didn't care.
I was already halfway down the hall.

ALL RIGHT ARLENE CALM DOWN I laughed back from the safety of my study with the sturdy lock and solid fireproof door to save me.

Just a normal day here.

Anyway Friday morning she walked into the kitchen carrying her breakfast dishes.
I was sitting there.
She plonked her dirty cup and plate and cutlery down right in front of me.
And declared that she was going to pee.
And gave me a smirk as if to say 'what are ye going to do now BertieAhern?'
What are ye gonna do now?
Go ahead Bertie.
Make my day.

And you know something?
I didn't have anything.

Well played Arlene.
Well played.

There is a nice wee priest on Tipping Point.
Father Tom.
Deadly.

Q1 was on a film about aliens. Little fellas from the sky. Not sure of the church attitude on little fellas in the sky, but he got it right.

Q2 was on sport. Rugby league. He doesn't strike me as a rugby type. He got it wrong.

Q3 was on beer. He got it right. Hmmmm Father, people will talk

Q4 classical music. The Pastoral was by which composer? Has to be a fix. He got it right. Of course he did.

Q5 was on trains. He looks like a train spotter. He got it wrong. Shocker.

Q6 Board games. Ah here lads. All those wild nights in the seminary paid off.

£3850.
The jackpot counter is hanging on the edge.
Will he gamble?

He does!!!
He gambles!!!
Go ahead Father. Ya rascal.

AND HE GETS IT ON THE SECOND COUNTER.
Celebratory priestly jump.
The communion wine will take a battering tonight, extra dollop of incense in the thurible, new alloys for the Toyota Starlet, and a few pounds in the Trocaire box.

Nice one.

Frank wanted a dog.
The wife didn't like dogs.
Frank loved Alsatians.
She thought it was a waste of money.
Frank found an Alsatian pup that was cheap because he had an extra toe on his left foot.
She said no.
Frank bought the pup and brought it home knowing that she would fall in love with the wee deformed pup.
She sort of fell in love.
The pup was staying.

On one condition.
Frank got to keep the dog, she would get to pick the name.
Frank gladly agreed.

Then she called the dog Tiddles.

A couple of years later and Tiddles got big.
Huge.
Massive.
So big that Police dog handlers in North Belfast used to cross the road to avoid walking past Tiddles.
That's how big Tiddles got.
But Frank couldn't bring himself to call the dog Tiddles.
He called it Tiddles in the house in front of the wife.
She called it Tiddles in the house too.
But outside the house he called the dog Titan.

Sit Titan.
Heel Titan.
Good boy Titan.

And Tiddles would look up at him as if he was a complete feckin eejit.
Who the feck is this Titan fella?
And then Frank would lean down and whisper 'good boy Tiddles'

Anyway.

One day Tiddles got off the lead in the Waterworks Park.
And Frank had to chase him to catch him.
Heel Titan he commanded.
Sit Titan he shouted.
HERE TITAN he roared.
To no avail.

And finally just as the dog was about the exit the gate to the busy Antrim Road Frank gave in.

HEEL TIDDLES he bawled.

And Tiddles immediately came to heel.

Anyway.
North Belfast being North Belfast the story got round.
Schoolkids used to say hello to Tiddles on their way past.
It drove Poor Frank mad.
Bus drivers used to beep at Tiddles.
It drove Frank crazy.
Police Dog Handlers still crossed the road, but this time towards Tiddles.
They would say Morning Frank.
Morning Officer.
Morning Tiddles.

FECK AFF OFFICER.
Sorry Frank, sorry Tiddles.

And poor Tiddles with the funny foot never knew what all the fuss
was about.

Morning all.
Isn't life grand?

21 Apr 2020, 10:16

I got a call.
A wrong number.
A strident, aggressive, shouty English lady, looking for a local hotel,
who happen to have a telephone number fairly close to mine.

That's grand.
It happens.

I started to explain she had a wrong number, but she started to
shout about diverting calls and people not answering and what sort
of a two bit operation were we running.

Even though it's not my hotel I felt this was a bit harsh.
So I told her that.

Then I started to explain that my only connection to that local hotel
was calling in for a pint on an occasional occasion but other than
that I had no connections, but she shouted even louder and
threatened me with all sorts about bringing me to court over some
drain cleaner and industrial supplies.

Even though it's not my hotel, I felt sorry for my staff having to deal
with such naked aggression.

I started to explain that she definitely had the wrong person but she started to yell about my people not doing their jobs and her being passed from pillar to post and how she wasn't accepting that from anyone any more

Even though it's not my hotel I snapped back.

And I told her that her drain cleaner was shite and the drains are still blocked and if she wanted paid she could just she come down and sort the drains out herself.
She blew a fuse and really started yelling that she just would do that.
I shouted fine and that I would get the toilet brush ready and slammed the phone down.

Ok I didn't slam it.
I don't do slamming.
But I definitely placed it in the cradle aggressively.

Anyway I'm off.
I'm away to my hotel to watch the shenanigans.
Should be good fun.
Mad English woman who can't dial numbers or listen to people is coming to clean my drains for me.
Still.
It will put the day in rightly.

PS. The more you shout, the less you get.

22 Apr 2020, 12:09

Last week she washed the floors and I wasn't allowed on them and I was stuck on the carpeted areas of the house.

Now she has washed the drive.
And the paths.
And the decking.
And I can't go outside.

Looks like I'm going to be indoors for a while.

I could be in serious trouble if she hoovers the carpet.
I might end up in the attic.

24 Apr 2020, 08:55

I was feeling good.
I was looking well.
Black trainers.
Black bottoms.
Black top.
Tanned face.
Comfortable.
And I just was feeling good.

Until a client walked in.

Looked me up and down
Looked at the black clothes.
Looked at the scrawny legs.
Looked at the midriff.
Looked at the shoulders.
Looked at the tanned face.
Looked at the grey hair.

Feck me big man, he said,
Every time I see you, he declared,

You look more and more like a pint of Guinness!!!

Morning all. Isn't life grand?

I did a post last month warning of the dangers of these Phishing competitions to win an RV or 250 TVs from Argos or a Range Rover that the previous winner was under 18, a holiday, £250 vouchers from Lidl etc. The sites were all set up very recently, had only one or two posts, these posts had been liked thousands and thousands of times. They are used to gather information.

I have seen some comments stating that they do no harm, people might as well enter, etc, etc.

So I'm sharing, with permission from the victim but without permission to tell you real names, what actually did happen to someone I know.

Jack, family man, business man, won a like and share competition on Facebook to win a brand-new Range Rover Evoque. A company called PV Competitions. Site set up the previous week. 40k likes. And Jack had won.
They phoned him to tell him.
He was sceptical.
He asked how much of a deposit did he need to send.
They assured him he didn't need to send a deposit, and told him never EVER to send a deposit for the like of this, all of those are scams!!!. The caller hated those scammers!!
Jack relaxed a bit.
But only for a second.

He asked how much was the delivery charge was.

Let me guess he says, £200?

NO the caller responded.

Don't ever EVER send a delivery payment, all of those a scams!!!

We don't do that, but we do need you to come to Liverpool to pick up your new car.

Jack relaxed more.

Now, said the caller.

Bit of housekeeping.

Here we go, Jack thought.

Publicity, the caller said.

We need your permission to take and use photographs or you and your family when you pick up the car.

OK, Jack said.

Great the caller said.

I will email over the contract.

Is that it Jack said?

That's it, the caller replied.

Sign the documents and send them back to me, I will get the car ordered and it will be here in a couple of weeks. Book your flights over and ferry home, arrange the insurance, and off you go.

WOW Jack said.

I have really won a car Jack said.

Yes Jack the caller said.

Congratulations

The documents arrived, the documents were all official, the documents were signed, the documents were sent back. The website looked good, it was a legitimate company, it seemed to have access to a lot of stock.

WEE TIP FOR YOU. If you start by getting people to agree to something small and easy, then something slightly less small, then

something else, when it comes to the big thing, they will be conditioned into saying yes. Trust and habit will have been established. It's easy to say No. It's harder to say yes, yes, yes, and then change to NO.

Jack got a call a week later.
Same lad.

After a period of congratulating and talking of plans with the new car and family and colours, the caller made a suggestion.
Now Jack he said.
You have won an Evoque, but they are a small car. You have a big family. Would you not trade it up to a Range Rover?
Jack agreed this would be nice, and the caller somehow made it seem that this was Jacks idea all along.
The caller said it wasn't really allowed, but he would see what he could do.
The caller would stick his neck out.
They were now pals.
He told Jack to go to Charles Hurst Landrover in Belfast, don't mention the competition win obviously, and test drive the Evoque and the big Range Rover and see which one he likes.
But don't let on about the competition, otherwise the caller will get in bother with the Range Rover network.
Jack agreed.
They were now partners in crime as well as pals.

Jack did this, he liked the bigger car, he loved the bigger car, he wanted his new best pal to sort out a bigger car.
The link on the PVCompetitions website stated that they had access to all these cars, new and used, so Jack selected one and rang his best pal.
His best pal could sort it out, the price difference was £11500 for a nearly new Range Rover. It was NOT to be paid now, it was to be

paid on the collection date. Anyone that asks you to pay now is a scammer. Don't ever pay in advance the caller told him.
Jack agreed totally.

An hour later the call came through that the car was now his, and it was marked as sold on the dealer website.
Jack was delighted.

Documents arrived to sign that he owed £11500, but no balance was payable until he had the car.
He signed them and sent them back.

Notice that you start by agreeing to small things, and it gradually builds. It's easy to say No. It's harder to say yes yes yes NO. And if you become cohorts, conspirators, comrades, it's quite difficult to say NO. And they were now cohorts.

A delivery date was agreed, Saturday morning for biggest Social Media exposure. Jack booked the flights.
Jack received pictures of the car being prepared, and a mechanics video. The caller kept in touch and seemed to be almost as excited the Jack. He kept telling Jack this was one of his biggest ever wins and he had been with PV Competitions for a year. The rest of the staff in the office were very jealous of him. The excitement was building.

On the Friday before he collected the car the caller had to arrange the money. He gave Jack the bank details and assured him the payments took 3 days. If there was any problem Jack could claim it back Monday morning. He had seen the car on site, and it was beautiful. He hoped Jack would take him for a spin round the block, and would it be OK it they all went for lunch before Jack left with the car?

Jack agreed. They were mates, and cohorts going out to lunch.

The money was sent.
Jack and family dressed to the nines and flew over.
They got a taxi to the address.
There was a name plate for PV Competitions on an office near the docks, but nothing else.
The phones weren't being answered.
The money was gone.
While they were there another taxi arrived.
They reckoned there were 5 taxis arrived that day.

Jack said the worst thing was his child's face.

The second worse thing was that one family had flown in to pick up their bog standard Range Rover, no deposit paid, nothing. The scammers hadn't got a penny out of them, but still let them fly over in the belief they had won a car.

Jack never got a penny back. He reckoned the scammers netted in excess of £50k that day for a couple of weeks work. And next week will be a different wee office and a different glossy website and different families.

So please check it out before you like and share. If it was set up yesterday with one post and 40k likes, it's a scam. And if you are going to tag people, please don't tag anyone you like. These scammers are very, very good at what they do. Don't give them access.

Morning all.

Stay safe.

Lads.
Urgent!!!
I need help.

We need a hairdresser.
Urgently!!!

The wife with the longer hair is starting to look very like the mother-in-law.
Very like her.
Scarily like her.

Please help.
Please.

Ah lads.

Living your life in fear of making a mistake is a huge mistake.

You are going to make mistakes.
You have made them in the past.
You are making them currently.
And you will make them in the future.

That's life.

Roll with them.

Learn from them.
Apologise if need be.
And move on.
But please don't berate yourself too much if you make another mistake today.

Morning all.
Isn't life grand???

6 May 2020, 07:26

I got a call today from Perth.
At least, that's what the phone said when the number came up.
A call from Perth.
I've heard of Perth.
It's in Australia.
So I answered in Australian.

GDAY MATE I answered.
Oh hello, came the posh Scottish lady replying.
Could I speak to someone about the professional indemnity insurance, she asked?
AH ITS A SHEILA, I declared.
WHATS THE WEATHER LIKE DOWN UNDER IN PERTH SHEILA, I asked?

She seemed surprised.

Oh, I'm in Perth in Scotland, I'm not actually down under, she replied.
DONT THINK SO SHIELA, I replied.
CHECK OUTSIDE, I ordered.
PHONE SAYS PERTH, I confirmed.
IVE BEEN TO PERTH, I declared.

ITS DEFINITELY IN OZ, I decided.
FAIR DINKUM SHIELA, I concluded.

No, there's a Perth in Scotland as well, she replied, and tried to get back on track about insurance.

STREWTH, I replied.
AND I SUPPOSE YOU ARE GONNA TELL ME THAT KYLIES A KIWI, I chuckled.

She hung up.

Don't know why.
Sheila must be a Kylie fan.
Pity.
I liked Sheila and her Insurance.
Anyway.
It puts the day in.
If I'm taking Australian for the rest of the week, you will know why.

CATCH YA LATER, THIS BRUCE IS GONNA BAIL!!!!

6 May 2020, 22:03

Isn't it amazing how often the truth is somewhere in between?

8 May 2020, 09:37

You ever notice that when you are climbing up a hill, the closer you get to the finish line, the harder you find it?

Yeah?

Doesn't it follow that the harder or tougher or more difficult something is, the closer to you are to the finish line?

I think so.

Keep going.

Better times are ahead.

#darknessintolight

9 May 2020, 17:09

I have this friend, who you wouldn't know, whose wife, who you also wouldn't know, fell out with him.

And all he did was stick up for one of her friends, who you incidentally also don't know.

Women eh?

His wife said her mate had to self-isolate because she had a bad chest.
And he said he thought she had a good chest
And the wife said no, she actually has quite a bad chest.
And he said he thought she had a luvly jubly soft cuddly warm bouncy chest.
And the wife said WHAT?
And he said he had always secretly admired her friends chest from afar.
And now, for some strange reason, the wife isn't talking to him.

Unbelievable.

Glad it wasn't me.
Women eh?

Morning all.
Isn't life grand?

11 May 2020, 07:49

I was making breakfast.
I was looking forward to it.
I had been dreaming about it all night.
It would be perfect.
It would be bliss.

It was all going well.
I poured two mugs of tea.
The toast popped just as the poached eggs were ready and the
veggie roll was reaching crispy juicy nirvana.
Quick butter, quick sprinkle of cheese, soft eggs delicately placed on
top, veggie roll artistically and lovingly positioned.

Then a minor issue.

I went to open the milk, but dropped the lid.
It went straight into a mug of tea.
I went to fish it out but it sank and the tea burned my fingers.
I sucked my fingers and used my other hand to lift a knife and fish it
out.
The knife had butter and crumbs on it.
And the tea now had butter scum and bread crumbs floating on it.
I noticed the Hells Bells had her back turned, so I put another dash
of milk in the tea to make it milky.
She likes her tea milky.
She would take the milky one.

I would get the perfect one.

I had restored the parity.
Go me.

I went to put the knife in the sink, HB went to lift her breakfast and her tea.

But she looked at the two teas.
And she took my strong, toast free, butterless tea instead.
And left me the scummy one.

Ah well.
Making another mug of tea would have been an admission of defeat.
Hope the HB enjoys her brekkie.
There's always tomorrow for me.

12 May 2020, 10:54

Memory from last year.

I know I rhyme on a bit about this stuff, but that's only because its important.
Especially important to the clever among us.
And to the creative among us.
And to the caring among us.
In other words it's important to the best people among us.
The best people are the ones most at risk.

People think that good mental health means that you are happy all the time.
It doesn't. You aren't.
It means that you are able to cope with the shite days when they

come.
And they will come.
It means you are able to enjoy the good days when they come.
Because they too will come.

People think that poor mental health means you are sad all the time.
It doesn't. You won't be.
It means you are less able to cope when the shite days come calling.
And they seem to come more frequently when you are less able to cope.
It also means you are less able to enjoy the good days when they come.
And they too seem to come less frequently when you are less able to enjoy them.

So I wish you good mental health this week.
And every week.

You will have shite days. We all do.
But you will cope.
And you will have great magnificent wonderful brilliant fantastic exotic erotic unreal absorbing astonishing unbelievable days too.
And they will be bloody marvellous.
Absolutely bloody marvellous.
Brace yourself.
They are coming.

It's OK not to feel OK.
Just remember better days are coming.

13 May 2020, 08:39

Myself and the daughter are working.
It's a necessary job.
Social distance rules being fully observed.

I fancied some breakfast.
I needed some breakfast.
So we stopped at Applegreen.
And we went in.
And we ordered.
Sausages beans and toast for me.
She just got snacks.

But the server put it in a takeaway box.
I was sort of curious, because the toast didn't fit, but she squeezed it in, and balanced the lid precariously on top. I didn't ask.

Then the tea.
It too was put in a takeaway cup, presumably because the breakfast was in a takeaway box.
I still didn't ask.

Then I went to sit down.
Only to find that the seating area is closed.
And I am standing with a tray, cutlery, a takeaway box and a takeaway cup.

So I did what any sane person would do.
I took the whole lot with me.
Tray and all.

For some reason the daughter is wetting herself laughing at me while being cross with me at the same time.

Women eh?

14 May 2020, 10:15

Tesco pickup day.

She orders online.
She picks it up.
We unpack.
We pack it away.
It's now dinner time.

She looks at me.
I look at her.

What do you want for dinner says me?
I got chops she says.
And spuds. And veg. And chicken. And a nice pie. And frozen fish.
And frozen veg. And burgers. And onions. And mince. And sausages.
And bacon. And eggs. And bread. And milk. And lasagna. And wine.
And cheese. Fridge and freezer are both full she says. Full to the
brim she says.

I look at her.
She looks at me.

So what do you want for dinner says me?

Chinese she says.

Sound perfect says me.

Shure, isn't life grand??

18 May 2020, 10:48

GREAT NEWS!!!!

Golf courses open from tomorrow.

BETTER NEWS!!!!

Weight Watchers and Slimming World stay closed.

It's been a good day all round lads.

18 May 2020, 17:51

The Hells Bells wakes up.
The Hells Bells checks Twitter.
The Hells Bells tells me about a funny tweet from the Wee Sister.
I check Twitter.
The tweet was very funny and sweet and made me smile.
I like a few tweets.
I comment once on a tweet.
I realise I have no idea how Twitter actually works, or what is
actually going on.
I'm a newb.
A muggle.
A virgin.
I'm waiting for people to finish their tweets, but they don't.
That's it.
That one wee bit.
That's all they have.
I can't cope.
I leave Twitter.
I go back to Facebook.
And I relax.
I feel at home here.
My Facebook.
Where life is normal.

Morning friends.
Isn't Facebook grand?

23 May 2020, 09:52

Many years ago I was in a tax inspection with a client.
He handed in his books.
The inspector flicked through them.
What's this he asked?
Takings, the client replied.
And this he asked?
Cash purchases, the client replied.
And this he asked?
Cheque and DD purchases the client replied.
The inspector flicked to the back of the book.
And finally this he asked?

It turned out to have been undeclared cash sales, names, dates and amounts that the client had helpfully written in the back of the book so that he wouldn't forget, but thinking that no one would ever check there.

Complete surprise to me.
Wonderful surprise for the inspector.
I conceded defeat.
With as much grace as I could muster.
It was the only course of action available to me.

Anyway.
Watching Boris and Dominic Cummings and their ridiculous attempts to defend the completely indefensible reminds me of how I felt that day.

Morning all.
Isn't life grand??

27 May 2020, 08:25

I was in the study, working away.
The Hells Bells came in.
She was talking on her mobile, hands free.
She waved at me.
I looked up at her.
She held up two fingers.
Then she did the walking thing with the two fingers,
And she thrust her hips at me, and did a funny face.

Jaysus Hells Bells, I thought.
I'm far too busy for any of that stuff, I thought.
At half three on a Thursday afternoon, I thought.
This lockdown has put her away, I thought.
She's gone a bit funny, I thought.

My face must have displayed my bewilderment.
She realised I was confused.
She attempted to clarify the seetuation.

She held up two fingers to me again.
I get it, me and you, I get it.
I nodded my assent.
Then she did the walking thing again.
I get it, me and you are going somewhere, I get it.
I again nodded my assent.
Then she thrust her hips at me again, and did a funnier face.
I did a stern face back.
NO, I replied.
JUST NO.

She appeared to now be confused, but she shouldn't have been. I'm a person, with thoughts and feelings and sensitivities. I don't want to be summoned and thrust at, I want to be cuddled, maybe held and definitely wooed. No woman will ever click her fingers at me and demand some thrusting.
That's why I said NO.

Hold on, she says down the phone.
Exasperated.

She turned to me.

She held up two fingers again.
WE she said.
I nodded my agreement. I had figured that bit out.

She did the walking thing.
ARE GOING she said.
I nodded my agreement. I had figured that bit out too.

Then she thrust the hips at me and did the funniest face of all.
TO THE CHIROPRACTOR she declared.

Ah.
OK.
That's grand then.
Work away Hells Bells.

I'm actually disappointed now, truth be told.

Ah well. There's always tomorrow.

Afternoon all.
Isn't life grand??

28 May 2020, 17:29

I had it all worked out, so I did.

We had a BBQ last night, and have stuff left over so i was going to make some scrambled eggs and microwaved sausages for breakfast.

Handy, so it was.
Unedifying, tasteless, unappetising but handy.

But then I remembered there were only 2 eggs left, so there were.
And we would need 4 eggs.
So I would need to go to the shop.
And while I was there I might as well treat us to a nice breakfast.
A nice soft sausage, hash brown, cheese and ketchup bap.
I could almost taste it.
The warm juicy sausage.
The crispy hash brown.
The spicy ketchup.
The cool cheese.
The soft succulent fresh bap.
I was salivating.
I could almost taste it.
My mind was made up.
I love it when a plan comes together.
This was going to be a good day.

On the way out the door i checked the fridge, so I did.
Just to see if we needed anything else.
And to justify the shop excursion.
So I could say we really needed bread and milk, but shure while I'm here.....

And found the eggs.
2 left in one packet.

But a full 10 unopened in another packet.
And bread.
And milk.
The Hells Bells had been shopping.

No excuse now.
Microwave it is then.
Bollox.

2 Jun 2020, 09:46

I'm doing accounts.
Its accrual world.
Calc you later.

Sometimes I am so funny; I just crack myself up.

3 Jun 2020, 20:50

Can I ask you something?
Respectfully ask.
Nothing aggressive.
Nothing accusing.
Nothing demanding.
Just a request.

Try to stop using the term 'committed suicide'
People do not commit suicide.
Try to say 'died by suicide' instead.
If you must.
Or 'bereaved by suicide'.
If you must.

Or something similar.
If you must.

But I honestly hope you never have to use any of those terms.

The term committed is outdated.
It adds to misinformation.
It adds to the stigma.
It adds to the alienation of those suffering from depression, anxiety or poor mental health.

Crimes are committed.
Sins are committed.
Suicide is not committed.
Suicide is suffered.
We need to support those who suffer.
We don't need to condemn them.

As I say this is just a request.
It's not a demand.
It's not an order.

It's OK not to feel OK.

Take care folks, tough times out there.

3 Jun 2020, 21:53

I went for a serious walk yesterday.
I gave myself a talking to as well.
I told myself to stop feckin about.
I needed to concentrate.
A pep talk.

No strolling, pump it out, I said to me.
OK, I replied.
And no saying hello and stopping to chat, I said to me.
OK, I replied.
And no petting of other people's dogs, I said to me.
What about other people's wives, I replied?
I thought I was funny, but serious me was having none of it.
Serious me gave a withering look.
And no whistling, concentrate on the job in hand, I said to me.
I raised my eyebrows doubtfully.
OK, I will try, but that one's going to be tough, I replied.

Selfies, I asked?
There's that withering look again.

I'm not sure I like serious me, but off we went.

And we walked fast, and we pumped it out, and we didn't say hello,
and we didn't whistle, and we tackled the hills with gusto and we
didn't dilly or we didn't dally.
We didn't particularly enjoy it either.
But we did it.

Back to the car.
Sweating, gasping, sore, legs knackered, wee toe blistered.
Glad it's over.

Then while I was on the way home wee daughter phoned.

Daddyyyy?
Yes pet, says me.
Fancy a walk?

I tried, but not even serious me can say no to wee daughter.

But stuff it.

A chance for a stroll and a chat and a giggle with the wee daughter?
I will take it.
Every time.
And I even got to whistle.

5 Jun 2020, 09:22

The Hells Bells was looking at me.
She had a look of desire on her face.
A look of wanton lust.
A look of unsatiable desire.
She wanted me.
She wanted me there and then.
She wouldn't take no for an answer.
The heat was rising.
I could see it.
I could sense it.
I could feel it.
A fool could feel it.

Big Don still has it.
Wanton desire.
It never left me.
It's nice to have a lady look at you like that.
Nice wee boost to the ego.

I decided to play it cool.

U all right there pet says me?

She quivered.
She bit her lip.
She licked her lips.
Her mouth was dry.

She stared at me.
Passionately.
Intently.

And then she spoke.
Quietly.
Pleadingly.
Achingly.

There is a white head on that spot on your neck she said.
I really want to squeeze it.

Yep.
Still got it.

6 Jun 2020, 11:59

I'm a snowflake apparently.

I get offended by things.
That's true.

I'm offended by bigotry. From any side.
I'm offended by sexism. From any side.
I'm offended by racism. From any side.
I'm offended by violence. From any side.
I'm offended by discrimination. From any side.
I'm offended by sectarianism. From any side.
I'm offended by hatred. From any side.
I'm offended by xenophobia. From any side.

However, people who call me a snowflake seem to be ambivalent
about the above.

And I find that offensive too.

Morning all.
Looks like snow here.

I was talking to an agency nurse working in a care home.
I asked her how she was getting on.

The answer was not good.

The care home she works in has lost five residents with the virus.
One lady died in her sleep.
The staff between themselves made sure that the other residents
had someone with them as much as possible in their final hours.
So the other four had some companionship.
It was the least they could do.
Family visiting was severely restricted.
The nurses wouldn't let them pass alone.
Where possible.

But she says.

It's not the same she says.
We have to wear masks and gloves she says.
We can't even offer the smallest of human touches she says.
And these people are our friends she says.
We have known many of them for several years she says.
We are very fond of them, she says.

It made me proud.
And it made me sad.
This lady is doing as much as she possibly can, and being

disappointed in herself that she can't do just a little bit more.
That made me proud.
Meanwhile other people are doing as little as possible, and
whinging and moaning about the little they have to do.
That made me sad.

This lady tested positive, she had to self-isolate for 14 days, no
contact whatsoever with her husband or her children for 14 days.
As soon as she got cleared, she spent a day with her family, and
next day went straight back to work. She missed her wee residents.

That makes me proud. And sad.

18 Jun 2020, 09:17

Mid March.
Compassionate.
Don't cry love, I know we are going into lock down, but you will see
everyone soon enough. Oh, you are crying for the hairdresser? Yes
love, I will miss her too......

End of March.
Examination.
Nope love, I can't see a single grey hair, and I'm looking very
closely.....

Mid April.
Resignation.
OK pet, maybe the slightest merest hint of barely noticeable grey
tingeness right down at the roots, but you can't see it unless you
look REALLY closely.....

End April.
Truthful

The difference between a bad haircut and a good hair cut is two weeks, but I think that only applies when its cut too short.....

Mid May.
Black humour.
What do you call a bee on a bad hair day?? A FRIZZbee!! Get it? Get it? FRIZZbee......Why aren't you laughing sweetheart, that's a cracker??.....

End May.
Complementary.
You know that big hair makes you look like you have lost weight, after all an inch taller is a stone lighter..... OK love, put down the knife and nobody will get hurt......

Mid June.
Dishonesty.
No love, I really love your hair that way, it suits you. And your eyebrows. You look more natural and relaxed this way. You should keep that haircut even when this is all over. And no, you look nothing like Noel Gallagher did back in the day.....

19th June.
Liberation.
The hairdresser phoned.
Thank Goodness.

19 Jun 2020, 12:10

Tomorrow is Daddy's day Daddy.
Yes pet I replied.
We are going to make you your favourite breakfast Daddy.
Oooohhhh that will be nice pet I replied.
Cheesy toasted soda with sausage and beans Daddy.

Oooohhhh lovely I replied.
And a big strong mug of tea with the milk in last!!
You know me so well I replied.

She was delighted.
Then she paused.

Daddy?
Yes pet I replied?
You know the way you get up early and drive us all mad with your
pottering and banging?
Do I pet I asked innocently?
You do Daddy.
If you say so pet I replied dubiously.
See tomorrow Daddy?
Yes pet I replied.
Could you stay in bed to a decent hour to give us a chance to get up
and make the breakfast Daddy?
Even though its Daddy's Day pet I asked?
Yes Daddy. Even though its Daddy's Day.
OK pet I promised.

So here I am now, everyone asleep, and me wide awake.

Happy Daddy's Day to all the Daddy's who want to get up and go for
a walk or a game of golf or fix that bit of the decking and the wee
leak in the roof and maybe the outside tap but we can't because its
Daddy's Day and we have to stay in bed wide awake and wait for
everyone else to get up and make us breakfast because its Daddy's
Day.

Awww shure.
Isn't life grand?

I love this stupid town.

I was in a shop a couple of years ago, and the owner had gotten himself in trouble with the Police.
Well, sort of.
He had been plagued by a gang of kids coming in, running amok, threatening staff, stealing stuff and dumping it outside.
So he threatened a couple of them and possibly gave one of them a bit of a dig.
Then some parents got together and came to complain about his treatment of their darlings.
So he threatened a couple of them and possibly gave one of them a bit of a dig.
Then the Police came.
And he told them to sort of the bloody shoplifters or he would give them a bit of a dig too.
The Policeman was old school.
He took it for what it was.
He told the shopkeeper that if it happened again, he would be scooped.
Then he went to the parents and told the parents that their kids were little shits, and that if they ever nicked stuff again, they too would be scooped.
And all went quiet.
The shopkeeper became known as a bit of a nutter, to be avoided, and the kids stayed well away.

I was in the shop last week, and a homeless man came in and stole a sandwich.
The shopkeeper did nothing.
Absolutely nothing.
Apparently it happens by the same lad usually once every week.

The shopkeeper does nothing because the homeless man is stealing out of necessity.

The kids were stealing out of disrespect.
Big difference.

I love this stupid town and its seriously messed up but bloody brilliant mad ways.

22 Jun 2020, 11:59

There are good things about this lockdown too.

For example.
I've been humming a Westlife song that's stuck in my head for two whole days now, and nobody knows a thing about it.
But even worse than that
Its one of the extremely shite Westlife songs that was written by Ed Sheeran.
And nobody can hear me humming.

So thank you lockdown.
Every cloud and all that.

Afternoon all.
Isn't life grand??

24 Jun 2020, 12:53

Daughter came in to me.

Daddddeee she said, in that way daughters say Daddddeee when they want something.
Yes pet says me.

What you doing tonight she asked?
My heart jumped.
It's not often she asks me.
I don't see as much of her as I used to, now that she lives elsewhere.
She obviously has something planned.
Maybe me and her for a curry chip.
Maybe me and her to the driving range.
Maybe me and her for a hill walk.
I was delighted to be asked.
But I decided to play it cool.
Nothing much, I replied.

I was thinking about having some friends round she said.
My heart jumped.
A wee sesh, a night's craic, a few friends, maybe a barbie, maybe a sing song, just what the doctor ordered.
I was more delighted to be asked.
But I still kept playing it cool.
What friends i asked?

Just the squad she replied.
My heart jumped.
Lovely gang of nut jobs.
I'm fond of them all.
And the daughter was inviting me.
This was brilliant!!!
We haven't seen a lot of her recently, with uni, and exams, and living away, and her rushing here and us rushing there, so it would be nice to catch up.
But I still kept playing it cool.
Shure, you don't want me there cramping your style I said.

Oh no, it wouldn't be the same without big Don she declared!!
I was delighted.
Over the moon.

Ecstatic.
This would be amazing, spend an evening with the daughter, and
the squad, and I've genuinely missed her, and the big son too, it's a
big quiet house without them.
This would be epic!!
I decided to stop playing it cool.
I would love to pet, I declared.
Are you doing it in the flat I asked?
Or in your wee garden I asked?

She looked at me.
A wry look.
I know that look.

Dadddeee??

Uh oh.

We were thinking of doing it in your house Daddddeee....

Uh oh.

And I was thinking you could come in to say hello Daddddeee....

Uh oh.

And then you could clear off for the night Daddddeeee....

Ah well.
It was good while it lasted.

Love you Daddddeeee......
I know you do, wee daughter.
I know.

Wee daughter bounced in.

Hey Daddy she says.
I got you your wrap she says.
Sweet chilli chicken and salad and a wee bag of Nordie Tayto as a
wee treat for my favourite wee Daddy she says.
And off she bounced.

So I opened the wrap and started to eat.
And it was rank.
It was a strange colour.
It was sweet and spicy and horrible and the salad was miniscule and
couldn't be seen.
It was the weirdest sweet chilli chicken I had ever tasted.

But the wee daughter got it for me.
And I don't like to disappoint the wee daughter.
So I decided to grin and bear it.

And I ate as much of it as I could bear without being sick.
Which turned out to be most of the chicken and the middle bit of
the wrap far away from the horrible sweet chilli sauce.
It was gross.
I can still taste it.
I'm retching even thinking of it.

Then wee daughter bounced in.

Hey Daddy she says.
Funny story she says.
I think I've got your sweet chilli chicken salad wrap, and you've got
my chipotle chicken wrap with no salad she says.
Was there salad on your wrap she says?

And the big eyes gazed at me innocently.

Oops.

Ahhh the old marching season here in Nordie land.
It's a funny time up here.
The only way to describe it is to use an example.

You know the way you go to the loo at half 10, like you always do.
With the newspaper under your arm, like you always have.
And locking the door, like you always do.
For 10 or 15 minutes down time, alone time, thinking time, like you always need.

And you relax.

And then 2 minutes later you hear footsteps.
Coming towards you.
Running footsteps.
Short stride, running footsteps.
Clicky heeled, short stride, running footsteps.
Female, clicky heeled, short stride, running footsteps.
Urgent, female, clicky heeled, short stride, running footsteps.

And you are sitting there, just minding your own business, having your wee bit of alone time, catching up on the sport then the problem pages then the news, safely behind a locked door.

But you know that in a couple of seconds there will be ructions as a very desperate, currently highly strung female who usually leaves it to the very last second of the very last minute to pee runs headlong into the door because its locked, and no amount of negotiation or pointing out the obvious or any request for consideration of your needs will persuade her or enable her to divert to another loo.

But it's all still a bit of craic.
And the door is still locked.
With you still inside.
Until the bricks get thrown.

Anyway. That's my impression of the marching season.
But don't mind me.
I'm in the loo.
With the door locked.
Finishing the paper from this morning.
Humming either The Sash or Sean South, I can never tell those two apart.

Afternoon all.
Isn't life grand?

6 Jul 2020, 17:05

Funny day today.

Family firm.
Youngest son.
Does the books.
Desperately wants to be in sales, but no room there, and he is too valuable where he is.
So he does the books and waits.
It will be a long wait.

Then I said the wrong thing to him.
I said something that made him sad.
I picked up on his reaction.
I asked why the reaction.

He told me it was because in all the years his parents had never said anything like that to him before.
Ever.

I told him he had done a good job, and really well done.

That's all. He had never been complemented.

As I say, funny day today.
Stop being so busy lads.
Little things matter.

14 Jul 2020, 22:00

Many months ago, I was coming out the gate and met a lady in a jeep with a distinctive number plate. I was turning right, across her. She was turning right, across me. We had one of those you go, no you go, no you go, ok we will both go, STOP moments. She stopped, she smiled and she let me out. So, I smiled back.

A few days later we met at the same junction, and I returned the favour. She smiled and waved, and I waved back.

Since them we pass each other roughly twice a week at various points in the road. And we smile and we wave. Big smiles. Big waves. Like besties. If she is late, I tap my watch. She gave me the fingers for tapping my watch and doing a disapproval face. Once she was standing at the fence waiting for me and tutting at my tardiness. I had a right chuckle.

But I still don't have the foggiest idea who she is. Nor does she know who I am. I know nothing about her apart from her distinctive number plate, her car, and the size of her head. And vice versa.

Anyway.
This morning I met her on the road.
And I gave a big smile and a big wave.
But she barely acknowledged me.
But worse than that.
She looked caught.
She looked guilty.
She started to wave, but then she put her head down, and just gave a tiny wave with her hand on the steering wheel.

And then I noticed the man with her in the car.

That's why she didn't wave.
I appear to be her guilty secret.
I'm her wave buddy.
If she was to wave at me, he might ask who I was, and she would have to explain that she has no idea who I am, but that we are just wave buddies.
And he might get jealous.
Or he might start waving himself.
But it's not his thing, it's our thing.

So there you go.
That's my only issue today.
See you soon wave buddy.
Leave your man at home.
He spoils our vibe.

Morning all.
Isn't life grand?

16 Jul 2020, 10:56

I just fell out big time with a man because he kept using an offensive phrase.
I told him if that was his attitude especially considering his audience he would be better finding someone else.
I took a stance against the aggressors, the judgemental, the privileged proletariat, the purveyors of social inequality.
I told him the terminology was dated, derogatory, disgusting aggressive and highly feckin offensive.
I stood up, I was counted, I stuck it to the man.
I was proud of me.

You want to know what he said that was so offensive?

He was talking about things being bad, and his exact words were;

"It's all going south very quickly"

The bollox.

Choose your words wisely my friends.

Morning all.
Isn't life grand?

I met wave buddy this morning.

She waved.
A tentative, nervous wave.
She knew.
After last week, she knew.

I was tempted to play it cool, and make her work for it, before that wonderful powerful moment when I accept her apologies and wave joyfully back and she realises that I forgive her and we both accept that its each other we wave to, it's always been each other, and only each other.

However, that's hard to convey in the split second when she is going one way at 30mph and I'm going the other at 42mph.

So I just waved.
Stuff it.
Wave buddies are hard to come by.
A big cheery wave.
And she smiled.
And I smiled.
And we went our separate ways a wee bit brighter than before.

22 Jul 2020, 13:13

Funny day yesterday.

I stopped in Monaghan to fill the car. I filled it and went to pay, but there was a long queue. While I was working my way down the queue a frazzled lady with a few bits of shopping and an upset child in a supportive buggy appeared at the side, and then saw the length of the queue.
She muttered something under her breath. Oh crap or something like that.
I told her to go ahead of me, and I dabbed at the child.
She was surprised.
So was the child.
Mummy was grateful.
Mummy mouthed thank you, and stepped in front of me.
The lady behind wasn't happy, and made a 'don't mind us, we are waiting too' comment. I ignored her.

The comment from behind annoyed me.

But the surprise from the mummy in front at someone helping her a teeny bit worried me too.

Why should she be surprised?

Glad yes.

Grateful maybe.

But surprised?

A lady struggling with an upset child is surprised that someone gives her a teeny bit of lee way?

Surely that must be the most natural thing in the world?

Surely most people would do the same?

Surely we haven't got to that level of shithousery that we wouldn't give frazzled woman have a bit of lee way?

Well OK the lady behind me has.

But surely not the rest of us?

It started me thinking. That's never a good thing. I thought it was funny. Funny odd.

But anyway.

I made it to Fermanagh where we took two lads who struggle with normal life out for a spin on the boat, a soaking in the rain, and a chippy tea. Herself went to get the chips, I got sent for a bottle of ketchup and a bottle of hand soap. For the craic I decided to mix these up. The lads thought this was gas. The soap went on the table and the ketchup went into the bathroom. The lads couldn't wait for the chips to come and the craic to start.

The chips came and the giggling started. Herself swapped the bottles over and the lads exploded when she slapped me. We calmed it down as the grub was served. But then they started giggling. I started chuckling and I couldn't look at them. They started laughing and couldn't look at me. I started crying and couldn't look at them. They started wheezing with laughter and couldn't look at me. I started to have problems breathing, so herself chucked me out because it had been half an hour and nobody had eaten. They started to calm down and eat so I put soap instead of ketchup on my plate. That started us off again. Then herself made me eat my chips dipped in soap, so i would learn my lesson. But I didn't learn it. And I suspect I never will. Because I like to make those lads laugh.

It's funny the craic you can have with ketchup, soap, and two lads with great bubbly laughs.

It's funny how you can give a tiny bit to people with special needs and get much, much more back.

It's funny how some people don't know that.

Morning all.
Isn't life grand?
I'm full of bubbles today.
Must have been the soap.

26 Jul 2020, 09:58

There are some things I am good at, some things I am capable at, some things I am experienced at. And there are also some things I'm not good at, not capable at, not experienced at.

Curiously, townies don't seem to have a problem with one of the things I struggle with.
Neither does the LGBT community.
It's just me, and all the other slightly autistic, sort of straight, severely culchie, painfully shy lads.

For 17 years I relied on me mammy for help.
Briefly I used to ask me sister.
For the last 30 years I relied on me wife.

And today one of those things came up.
But I had nobody to ask.
No mammy. No sister. No wife.
I was exposed.
Vulnerable.
Helpless.
Desperate.
Naked.
And I had to go it alone.

I went into the menswear shop.
They eyed me up and down.
They saw me for what I was.
They sensed my weakness.
They surrounded me.
They preyed on me.
I told them what I needed.
It didn't matter.
Nothing I said mattered.
First they told me I needed a shirt.
I denied this.
It didn't matter.
I ended up with one that if I lean forward slightly it fits perfectly.
I objected. It didn't matter.
Then another that is the same make, and will require the same stoop.
While I'm stooping, I might as well.
I fought back.
I told them that the wife would be cross at me stooping in an effort to halt the sale.
So I ended up with a third shirt that doesn't require a stoop, but that is apparently all the rage and the wife will love it.
There isn't a chance I will ever wear it, but the wife will love it.
I'm just not built for all the rage.
But I ended up with it.

Then they mentioned trousers.
And jumpers.

I grabbed the shirts and the one thing i went in for, and went to the
till and paid.
The one thing I went in for?
Underwear.
That's all I wanted.
Why is it so hard for an autistic, straight, shy, culchie fella to buy
underwear?

Ah well. That's me sorted for a while. If you see me stooping,
remember to complement the shirt. Its new. Don't mention the
pants. I'm shy about them.

PS I hope this isn't offensive to the LGBT community, mammy's,
wives or sisters. Its not meant to be. I would hate to offend anyone
on that list. Townies however can feck off.

Anyway. Isn't life grand?

30 Jul 2020, 21:46

We were heading out last night.
We had to get changed.

She did her make up.
She tried on a top.
She liked it.
She tried on trousers.
She liked them.
But she didn't like the trousers and top together.
So she changed the top.

Then she changed the trousers.
Then she changed back to the original top.
Then she was happy.

My options were limited.
I haven't been home in 9 days.
I had one shirt left.
I had shorts or trousers left.
Plenty of Lynx Africa.
Choice of trainers.

But I wanted to make an effort.
She had made an effort, I would make an effort.
So I decided to stick with the shirt I was wearing, the shorts I was wearing and the Lynx Africa, but change the trainers.
She would be impressed.
I would make her proud.

She looked me up and down.
She sniffed me.
She checked out the shirt.
She checked out the shorts.
She checked out the trainers.

I would change those, she says, pointing at the trainers.

Your other pair were tidier, she says.

Ahh well.
Hopefully she appreciated the effort.

2 Aug 2020, 10:16

Nice wee day yesterday.

Caught up with friends. And the female son in law. Nice breakfast, nice dinner, nice glass of wine, nice cycle, lots of fresh air and fun and chat.

Made a wake for the jet skiers to jump.

Encouraged other people's kids to jump off bridges just so I could get mid-air selfies.

Found where big son and his mates were doing some very strange turns mid lough according to the GPS tracker, turns that made pictures of male genitals. As you do.

Nice wee day.

Oh and explained quite politely but aggressively to a bully (I didn't realise that this could be done, but I do think I hit the mark) that some people are purely ignorant by nature, and other people are only ignorant when provoked. The insinuation was that the bully was ignorant by nature, whereas his victims had been provoked. Judging by the colour his neck went, he fully understood the insinuation. So did his friends. But he didn't have the integrity or the courage to stand up to me, but then I suppose I was quite ready and willing and able to stand up for myself. He prefers older unsure people and younger unsure people. I shall remember with fondness the angry colour that neck went for many a long day.

It's been a nice wee day.

Morning all. Isn't life grand??

10 Aug 2020, 09:50

Killarney.

Don she says.
Yes pet says me.
Which toilet is which she says?
What do you mean says me?
That one over there says Fir she says.
That's men says me.
And that one says Mmmmna she says.
That's for the women says me.

And I was glad to have helped.

But she looked at me sideways.

You are a liar she giggled.

I was insulted.
I protested my innocence.
I demanded justification.
I told her I would ask the people beside us.
She didn't trust them either.
I told her I would ask the waitress.
She denied this too.
She said she would just go up and see the picture on the door.
I pointed out that there were no pictures, just words Fir and Mna.

So she googled it.

And found out I was right.
I hadn't lied.
She could trust me.

But then she got cross because even though I hadn't lied, I had been proved right and she had been proved wrong.

Ah well.

Next time I will lie.
Keeps me out of trouble.

I'm colour blind.
I've always been colour blind.
I wasn't definitely diagnosed for years, but I had a fair idea.
My drawings at school had people with green hair, it wasn't exactly a surprise.
It also wasn't that important, I had many other quirks which required more urgent assessment.
But I was finally tested and told I was definitely colour blind when I was 17.
I've come to terms with being colour blind.
It's OK. It's all good.

Now I have been informed I'm not colour blind. I never was colour blind. There's no such thing as colour blindness.

I'm actually colour deficient.

It's just a whole new issue I now have to come to terms with.

Being called a blind eejit was OK. I'm not sure about being called a deficient eejit.

Morning all. Isn't life insufficiently deficient?

Awww the Nordies. Lovely people.

I walked into the house.
The Hells Bells was waiting.
The Hells Bells was in good form.
The Hells Bells was in great form.
The Hells Bells had shopping bags.
The Hells Bells had been shopping.
I asked her what she had bought.
She pulled out a bunch of flowers and waved them at me.
FLARES FER YER GRAVE she snarled.
FLARES FER YER GRAVE!!!!

Now.

Some people might be taken aback at this.
But I know the Nordies.
And that's actually an affectionate statement.
For a Nordie.
That means she is going to visit me when I'm dead.
That means that she will miss me when I'm gone.
Even if she is the one that kills me.

And that's about as sweet as a Nordie gets.

Morning all. I think I've pulled. You will love her. She bought me flowers. She's a Nordie.

17 Aug 2020, 08:47

It could happen to anyone.

I woke up early.
I couldn't go back to sleep.

I decided to do some work.
But I knew she would be cross.
Because I am on holidays.
But stuff needs done.
And my clients need me
And she just doesn't love my clients like I do.
So I snuck out of the room to do some work.

We good so far?

Ok then.

On the way I snagged my shirt, which incidentally is very, very
similar to the one Geoff Metcalf was wearing in Corrie last night. I
know he is a bullying asshole, and put his poor wife in jail, and
manipulates poor Tim and stuff like that but he does have good
taste in shirts.
Good man Geoff.
I however didn't grab my trousers, the pockets are full of coins and
car keys and they would jangle and wake her up and she would tell
me off for sneaking out.
I'm clever that way.

Anyway up I went and did an hours work but then got a touch cold.
But I still didn't want to risk wakening her.
So I took the throw off the sofa and wrapped it round me.
Like a sarong.
Like David Beckham wears.
Airy, and surprisingly comfortable, but very forgettable when
wearing.
And I went back to work.
Good man Becks.

But forget I was wearing it was what I did when I went out the
decking as a metrosexual man to have a biiiiggggg stretch and check
the weather, much to the undisguised disgust of the manly man

next door, but very much to the undisguised desire of his lovely womanly wife.

Ah well.
Morning Becks, Geoff, Neighbours, Clients and wife.
Isn't life grand??

18 Aug 2020, 11:00

Ahhh lads. I love this place. But sometimes this place drives me demented.

We decided to get a Chinese for dinner, and a bottle of Coke Zero. I went to pick it up.

I got the Coke Zero first in the Centra, mask on, hands squirted on, lifted a 2l bottle, £1.80. I handed the nice wee lad 2 quid, and told him to stick the wee change in the wee jar. All good. 20p donated to Concern, me improving my chances of getting into heaven, and a risk of contamination from the nice wee lad avoided.

I went to the Chinese, chicken curry and chips, honey chilli chicken and chips, chicken chow mein and a curry sauce, £20.20. I handed the nice wee girl a £20 note, and went searching for change.
But I found none.
Because I had donated it to Concern.
So I had to hand out another £20 note.

She looked at me dubiously.

Ohhh she said.
Have you any change she said.
No says me.
I gave it to Concern says me.

And I told her about the Coke Zero at £1.80 and the nice wee lad and the wee change in the wee jar.

She looked at me impressed.
She smiled at me.
I know him she says.
He is nice she says. (I think she liked him)
£20 will do she says.
Don't worry about the 20p.
Grand says me.
Thanks says me.
And I got the dinner, and left chuffed and cockahoop.

I love this place.

But then I realised.

I hadn't actually given Concern the 20p, had I?
I had meant to, but I hadn't.
The wee girl in the Chinese had.
So now the wee girl in the Chinese will be getting into heaven, and I will be left standing in the queue at the Pearly gates arguing with St Peter all because I was 20p short.

And that's why it drives me demented too.
There is a storm coming, we are in a pandemic, the wife has been stuck with me for months, I'm in constant danger, and now thanks to a nice wee girl in the Fermanagh Chinese I'm behind on my protection money.

Someone stick 20p with my name on it in a Concern jar please? Oh, and tell the nice wee lad in the Centra that the nice wee girl in the Chinese fancies him? Then we will all be back even again.

Bring on the storm.

19 Aug 2020, 18:49

Chilling at home, watching series 1 of Line of Duty.

I can only conclude from the behaviour, the language and the tone that somehow, someway many years ago Ted Hastings (like the battle) became my bride and since then somehow, someway he has given me 2 wonderful children.

So he did.

You never see him and the Hells Bells in the same room, do ye?

22 Aug 2020, 20:06

Nice wee moment yesterday. Maybe it translates. Maybe it doesn't.

Meeting people for the first time.
Nice people. Likeable people. Strident wife, quiet hubby.

He told her off for being a little too forthright.
I just call it as it is, she replied.
I just call a spade a spade, she declared.

Aye, he replied.
Even when it's a shovel, he declared.

I snorted with laughter, he grinned with delight, she smiled with an admission of guilt. Nice wee moment.

Hope you all had a nice wee moment yesterday too.

27 Aug 2020, 08:46

Depression. Anxiety. Poor mental health.

Some call it weakness. Maybe it's not weakness. Maybe its staying too strong, for too long, without help, while trying to carry the weight of everyone and everything on your back. Maybe it's being intelligent, and creative, and kind, but also being a little too self-aware, a little too self-critical, a little too over analytical.

But maybe it's not weakness.

True weakness is being trite, true weakness is not bothering enough to care, true weakness is not caring enough to bother, true weakness is risking nothing and achieving less, true weakness is aiming for ordinary and falling short, true weakness is being average, not being exceptional.

Accept your intelligence, your kindness, your creativity. Accept that some days are going to be tough, mainly because you are so tough on yourself. But that's OK. There's always tomorrow.

See you in the morning. We ordinary average people need you. We need you a lot. Take care.

31 Aug 2020, 21:18

I called in to Papas yesterday for a meeting, I was early, the other fella was late, but luckily I happened to bump into the local conspiracy theorist.
Now.
I enjoy him.
He spouts rubbish, but a lot of it is entertaining.

He is good value as they say.
You know the sort.
So I stopped to chat.

From him in the past I have learned that the earth is shaped like a disk, and claims that it is round are a plot by the Masons to destabilise the markets and then they can control the world.
School massacres in the USA never happened, the claims are a plot by the Liberals to destabilise the NRA and then they can take over the world.
The Holocaust never happened, and the claims are a plot by the Jews to destabilise our society and then they can take over the world.
Clouds don't exist, what we see in the sky is actually exhaust plumes from spy planes.
Your phone is spying on you. (Actually, that one is definitely true)
The moon landings did happen, but they had to re-enact the filming in Area 51 in Nevada because they couldn't show what they actually found on the moon. That's where the confusion comes in.

Anyway I was wearing my face mask.
And he was disappointed in me.
He assured me there is no virus, masks don't work, nobody has gotten sick or died, its a myth spread by the Chinese Socialists in league with the media and using the medical profession to spread fear and destabilise our markets, and then they can take over the world.

I decided to change tack.

I agreed with him. Totally. 100%. He was very surprised at this. Usually I poke fun, but today I was in agreement.

So then I leaned closer to him and I whispered that I told the doctors that very same thing Monday morning when they told me I had tested positive, and that the self-isolating order for 14 days they had imposed on me was pure bullshit designed to silence me, and that their claims that I would get Covid in 5 to 7 days was absolutely lies designed to spread fear. I would NOT be silenced.

And then I chuckled at my cleverness and their failed scheme, but he must have thought my chuckle was a cough because he recoiled from me quite quickly.

Ah well. I suppose he is a conspiracy theorist Covid denier, but he wasn't so definite when I actually putting the theory into practice. He wasn't ready to take that step.

I had breakfast, avocado, poached eggs and toast with gallons of tea, even though avocado is probably a plot by vegetarians to destabilise the Full Fry market and enable them to take over the world.

Ps. I haven't tested positive, I lied, but in my defence, he started saying stupid things so I thought I would just join in.

Morning all.
Just because you are paranoid doesn't mean they aren't out to get you.

3 Sep 2020, 11:37

I was told that if you didn't have a mask you could avoid Coronavirus by slowly exhaling as you walk past people. That way you wouldn't inhale the germs.

I was doing OK until I met that bus load of tourists........

4 Sep 2020, 12:46

I've a nice day ahead.
I don't think I can tell ye yet.
I'm sort of sworn to secrecy.
But it's a big treat and an honour and a privilege.

I told me mammy.
That goes without saying.
Swearing someone to secrecy doesn't include mammys.
Everyone knows that.
Mammys are allowed.
Mammy was proud.
Very proud.
I told her not to tell anyone.
She promised not to tell anyone.
Big secret.

Then I told my wee sister.
Now I know that swearing someone to secrecy doesn't include
mammys, but I'm not so sure that clause applies to wee sisters.
I was being bold.
But I told her.
I had to tell someone, I was bursting.

Oh I know, wee sister replied.
I was talking to mammy, she replied.
She told me all about it, she replied.
But it's OK, she replied.
She told me it was a secret, and not to tell anyone, she replied
laughing.

Morning all.
Isn't life grand?

9 Sep 2020, 07:19

World Suicide Awareness Day.
I've been honoured and privileged and lucky enough to meet President Higgins in the Aras.

#cycleagainstsuicide
#lightingthelight
#itsoknottofeelok

Your anxiety is lying to you. That's what anxiety does. Its lying. It's not telling you the truth.
Your depression is lying to you too. That's what depression does. It's not telling you the truth either.
Anxiety and depression are scummy, cowardly sneaky, bullying, liars.
That's all they are.

You only listen because you care enough to consider these things. You only listen because you are intelligent enough to be self-doubting. You only listen because you are creative enough to be self-critical.

Don't change. Don't stop caring. Don't hide your light.

Adapt.

Stop saying 'yeah, but the thing is....'
Don't say 'I want to go exercise, yeah but the thing is it's raining'.

Instead say 'yeah, but I'm still here....'
As in 'I may not have exercised enough, yeah, but I'm still here'

And smirk.
Don't shy away.
Don't hide.
Don't cower.

Look straight and deep at those dirty lying cowardly dishonest bastards that are anxiety and depression, and smirk.
And say 'yeah, but I'm still here'

You may have bitten me, but you haven't beaten me.
I'M STILL HERE.

10 Sep 2020, 10:19

I've been reading this past week about the people who refuse to wear masks and follow instructions. Their numbers are increasing. They are getting more vocal. This virus is all a myth and lies blah blah, we are all sheep blah blah, only they know the real truth blah blah, they read it on Facebook blah blah, and they won't be silenced blah blah.

Ok then.

I'm wearing a mask. I'm washing my hands. I'm disinfecting, I'm trying to keep my distance. I'm still out walking, I'm still out golfing, I'm still eating out occasionally, I'm still travelling when I absolutely need to, but I'm taking care.
Little things.
If the doctors are wrong, my actions mean I will look stupid, look at the state of me wearing a silly mask and washing my soft fairy liquid hands.
But that's OK.
I can cope with looking stupid.

You are not wearing a mask, you are not washing your hands, you are not disinfecting, you are not keeping your distance.
Little things.
If the doctors are right, your actions mean people will be at risk of infection, illness, and death.

And that's not OK.
I care about people. I worry about people.

So here's the thing.

If you are not willing to take small sensible steps to stop this virus, I don't want you near me, I don't want your work, I refuse to have any dealings with you. Take them elsewhere please. I wish you well, but this is my final decision. You have your rights, and I have mine.

Morning all.
Stay safe.

21 Sep 2020, 10:17

Met wave buddy the other morning, hadn't seen her in 3 months.
I got a big happy surprised wave from her.
That was nice.
I waved back. A big one.

This was immediately followed from her by a pushy arm outstretched 'where the feck have you been???' face.
Now, that wasn't just as nice.
Even wave buddy is giving out to me.
I bristled.
No woman has the right to give out to me.
Apart from the wife.
And the Mammy of course. Actually, the daughter too, the sister as well, some of the sister in laws, most of the wife's friends, a couple of the aunts, and the female son in law.
But that's it. No other woman can give out to me.

I did a wild, googly eyed, tongue stuck out, on the sesh, woohoo, pretending to swig from a bottle signal, to indicate that I've been

partying.
This seemed to make her mad.
Extremely mad.

But then she was gone. It's hard to have a meaningful conversation in sign language when she is going one way at 30 in a 30 zone, and I am going the other way at 47.

It may be partly my fault
My googly eyed, tongue out, bottle holding 'i was on the sesh' gesture could have been portrayed as 'I got done for drink driving'. Or indeed 'I'm currently drunk as a skunk while driving'. Or possibly 'I've been in an intimate month lockdown relationship with a particularly well-endowed man'. That could explain her reaction

Ah well.
Next time I will tap my watch and smile sadly.
Women are suckers for sad smiles.
If there is a next time.

23 Sep 2020, 11:30

Hey lads.
Times are tough.
It's hard.
Some people are struggling

So, why not try this.
See when you are talking to someone?
Or texting someone?
Or contacting someone?
Don't make it just business.
Take 2 mins.
Ask how they are.

How's it going?
What's the craic?
Or maybe give someone a call for no reason.
Or make up a reason.
Have a chat.
Talk shite.
Tell a yarn.

I reckon that what you say doesn't matter, the fact that you are saying something does.

For a lot of people that could be the only interaction they have that day.

Let's make it count.

As for me?
I'm grand.
A few people took a few minutes to chat with me today. To see if I was OK. Guess what? I was.
Or maybe I took a few minutes to chat with them. To see if they were OK. Guess what They? They were too.

Cheers lads. Little things matter.

24 Sep 2020, 21:21

I was booked to work in an office.
I drove up, as normal.
I parked outside, as normal.
I went in, as normal.
I sat down and waited for the boss there to finish, as normal.

The door opened behind me.

I glanced at the person coming in.
Human nature.
Just a glance.
He was a big man.
A naturally huge physically muscular man.
6 and a half feet tall.
3 and a half feet wide.
He had to crouch and turn slightly sideways coming in the door.
I turned away.

All normal.

Then he spoke.
He had slightly slurred, slightly stunted speech.
That's a quare sexy car you have there, he says.

The place erupted laughing.
But laughter with a strong tinge of derision.
It wasn't pleasant laughter. It was scornful laughter.

The boss beside me spoke.
Here, he says to me.
Lurch is talking to you, he says.
More snide laughter.

I didn't like that laughter. I didn't like that nickname.

I turned.
The big lad was looking at me.
He was uncertain. He was smiling, but it was a nervous smile. He didn't know much, but he knew enough to know he was the butt of the joke.
As usual.
And he didn't have the ability or the ammunition to fight back.
He was an easy target.
He didn't fit in.

As usual.

I didn't like that uncertain smile.

I decided that they had been slightly mean to the big lad.
I wouldn't be.

Cheers pal, I announced.
You like your cars, I asked?
He did.
You want to see it, I asked?
He did.
The nervous smile disappeared.
And off we went to see the sexy car.
For half an hour.
While everyone else waited.

The boss wasn't happy with me when we came back. He moaned about wages and payday and VAT to be done and stuff like that.
I just laughed at him.
With derision.

30 Sep 2020, 10:10

I was meeting up with a potential new client.
No obligation meeting.
Never met each other before.
Half 9, their place of work, I was suited and booted, clicky shoes, shifting shirt, dose of Lynx Africa, laptop and briefcase, raring and ready to go.

I arrived and rapped the door.
A lady answered.
Hello, says me cheerily.

I'm here to see Missus Soandso, says me.

She scowled at me.
A miserable judging unimpressed scowl.
You are early, she declared dourly.

I looked at my watch.
9.24am. I was indeed 6 minutes early.
I looked at her dour, sour, critical, judgemental face.
I thought about working with her.
I thought about dealing with her for the foreseeable future.
I thought about the possibility of us sitting side by side, our legs
almost touching, our heads bent together as we connected over an
elegant Trail Balance.
I didn't like what I saw.

Sorry, says me cheerily.
I will be back when I'm late, says me happily.
And I left.

She phoned several hours later wanting to know when I was coming
back, I told her that her work wasn't for me and my work wasn't for
her and thanked her for her interest.
And hung up before she could reply.
I might be a saint, but I'm no angel.
Sometimes life is just too short.

Ah well.
Shifting shirt back in storage.

1 Oct 2020, 15:18

I got up early this morning for a golf day.
Herself woke up.

Morning says me.
How are you says me?
I've a sore head she says.
Awww no, you want tablets says me?
I got some earlier she says.
Cup of tea says me?
No ta she says.
Anything says me?
I'm grand she says.

So off I went.

I was in Applegreen in Lisburn when I got the message that the golf
had been cancelled because of the weather.
So I turned and went home.

I came in the front door to the sound of her alarm going off. I went
upstairs to see how she was.
How you feeling says me?
I'm grand she says.
I took two tablets earlier, and now I'm grand she says.

And then she realised what time it was.

What about your golf she declared?
Did you not go she asked?

I thought quickly.
Footie on the tele, Scottish Open golf, Liverpool match this evening,
then PGA tour golf.
Brownie points could be useful.

Awww no says me.
I couldn't leave you says me.
I was worried about you says me.
I thought you had a migraine says me.

And I smiled sadly.

She looked aghast.
I feel terrible she says.
You shouldn't have missed golf for me she says.
It was just a headache she says.

Its grand says me, still smiling sadly but counting up all the brownie points in my head.

It was all going really well until she checked Facebook and saw the Golf Society post cancelling the golf ......

4 Oct 2020, 10:45

Nice day.
Funny day.
Quirky day.

I gave the Cooley wave to a Cooley man in Carrickfergus.
He appeared chuffed, but confused.
The Cooley wave is seldom seen outside of Cooley, you see.
I suspect there may be an inquisitive Hooley in Cooley to discuss.

I got the lights from a yoke behind in Ballynure to speed up.
I refuse to rush, you see.
And the lad behind flashed the lights, and gave a cheeky wee 'get on with it I'm in a hurry' wave.
I just laughed, mainly because he was in a John Deere Tractor, and I was in a car.
And it wasn't even a big John Deere, it was only a wee John Deere.
If she's green, she shouldn't be seen.
I sped up.
I was worried he would pull out and overtake.

Then I went to a clients to pick up books.
Odd lad, quirky lad, likeable lad.
Him, not me.
He wasn't there.
I called him.
I'm on the way, he says.
I will be there in.....
click click click.
6 minutes, 30 seconds he says.
I laughed.
Did you just put it into sat nav I asked?
He had.
6 minutes 30 seconds I asked?
It was.
I'm going to time you I said.
See if you can beat it I said.
You are on he says.
GO he yelled.
And beat it he did.
5 minutes 58 seconds.
I did a big Top Gear flourishing stopwatch finish as he went past and skidded to a halt.
He was chuffed at the time, and the flourish.
He claimed he would have been quicker, except there was a lad in a wee John Deere going slow in Ballynure.

Nice day.
Funny day.
Quirky day.

Culchie day.

7 Oct 2020, 21:24

Ever notice how we don't own things, things own us?
Maybe we don't own our cars, our car owns us?
Maybe we don't own our houses, our houses owns us?
Maybe we don't own that big TV, that big TV owns us?
Maybe we don't own that fancy phone, that fancy phone owns us?
Maybe we don't own that gaming console, that gaming console owns us?
Maybe we have it all wrong?

Maybe we should stop trying to own things?
Life is a list of achievements, not a list of acquisitions.
Try to achieve things, not acquire things.
Start small.
Work our way up.

Invest in ourselves.
Invest in our experiences.
Invest in our family
Invest in our friends.
Invest in walking.
Invest in holidaying.
Invest in fresh air.
Incest in water.
Invest in diet.
Invest in hiking.
Invest in cycling.
Invest in sharing.
Invest in caring.

Achieve things and experiences for us.
And stop trying to own things that really own us.

Morning all.
Isn't life grand?

It will be.

World Mental Health day.

Try something for me.
Please.

Go easy on yourselves today lads.
Give yourself a break. Just for today.
Stop second guessing yourself. Just for today.
Stop criticising yourself. Just for today.
Stop berating yourself. Just for today.

Forget about your mistakes. Just for today.
Everybody makes them.
Mistakes are bruises.
Anxiety is a bruise.
Depression is a bruise.
Bruise's fade.
And disappear.

If you are hurting mentally, it's because you are either intelligent or creative or kind.
No other reasons.
You are above average.
You are outstanding.
You are exceptional.
You are gifted.
Embrace those gifts. Just for today.

Stop trying to fit in with ordinary, when you are extraordinary. Just for today.

Try that. Just for today. One day. Let's be honest here, what have you got to lose? Please?

And see tomorrow?
Do exactly the same as you did today. Be a touch more positive.
About yourself.
To yourself.

And then next day.
Same again. Except it will be slightly easier. You will be getting used
to it.

And the day after?
You got it. Share it sideways. Keep it going.

And next week?
Next week thinking slightly more positive about yourself will
suddenly have become a habit. Making a small change for seven
days will make it a habit.
And habits are hard to break.
Sure, don't we all know that???
Aren't we walking proof of that???

By the way, you will still have bad days. Don't think you won't.
But you will be better able to cope with them.
And you will still have good days too.
But you will definitely be better able to enjoy those.

That's what people mean when people say it's OK not to feel OK.

And if you find yourself slipping, it's absolutely OK to ask for help.

Ok?
Yeah?
We agreed?
Good.

See you tomorrow.

Ad blue light came on.
Car started counting down.
I'm going to stop in 600 miles.
500 miles.
400 miles.
So I went to get ad blue.

First of all, ad blue isn't blue.
I felt cheated.
It's a clear liquid.
But that's 2020 for ye. Everything a bit of a disappointment.

Secondly I had to pour it into the spout beside the fuel cap while taking care not to spill it because ad blue is highly corrosive.

Daughter came out.
What you doing Dad, she asked?
I'm filling up the ad blue, says me.
What's ad blue, she asked?
It makes the exhaust gases cleaner, says me.
Ok, she says.
And she thought about it.
That's good, she says.
She watched for a second.
I was worried what you were up to, she says.

I waited for it.
I know her.
I know when there is something good coming.

Something worth waiting for.
And I there was something good coming.
I could feel it.
What were worried about, I asked?

Oh, I saw you with that tank, and I thought you were running that yoke on red or something, she declared.

Jaysus.
The daughter has gone all Culchie on me, I've never been as proud.
Running on Red!!!!

20 Oct 2020, 15:53

Bad scare earlier.
Nearly passed out in fear.
Couldn't taste anything.
Couldn't smell anything
I thought I had caught the virus.
I started thinking of who I had been in contact with, who I had infected, who had infected me.
I wondered about my temperature, I felt it could be high, I felt warm and I was definitely sweaty.
It was horrible.
Truly horrible.
A horrible, horrible feeling.

But I wondered why I didn't have a cough.
That made me pause.
That made me think.

I then realised that I was snacking on Nordie Tayto.
The yellow stuff.
Times are hard you see.

The border is closed you see.
Supplies of proper Tayto are running low for us Crisp Connoisseurs you see.
The penny dropped.

I am used to proper Tayto, not Nordie Tayto.

I hadn't lost my sense of taste and smell, Nordie Tayto is so bland there is no taste, nor smell, to start with.

That's what had fooled me.

Be aware lads.
Those Nordie crisps should come with a warning.
'So bland and tasteless consumers may experience similar symptoms to Covid'

Phew.
Wear a mask.
Wash your hands.
Keep your distance.
Avoid fake crisps.
Stay safe out there lads.
If we winter this one out, we can summer anywhere........

21 Oct 2020, 15:02

I got a phone call from a lovely lady in London wanting to do a survey about my clients banking arrangements.
Hmmmm.
Slightly suspicious.

Who for, I asked?
She said 'it's for M C Cann'

She didn't say McCann like I would say McCann all one word, she said the M C separately like in M C Hammer.
Who for, I asked?
Its for M
C
Cann, she said.

I giggled.
Giggles are good. Especially these days.

I pretended to think about it.
Let me think, says me.
And I hummed.
Doo do do do.
Do do.
Do do.
Let's do this, I declared emphatically.

She seemed quite happy, if slightly bemused.

What bank are M C Cann currently with, she asked.
I chuckled.
Chuckles are good. Especially these days.
I will check, says me.
I hummed again.
Doo do do do.
Do do.
Do do.
Cant tell you, I declared emphatically.

She seemed disappointed, if slightly concerned.

Are you happy with your banking arrangements at M C Cann she asked?
I laughed.
Laughing is good. Especially these days.

Let me think.
I hummed while chuckling.
Doo do do do.
Do do.
Do do.
Cant share this, I declared.

She hung up.
Maybe for the best.
M C Cann didn't think he would have been able to cope with
another question.
It made my day.

M C Cann in da HHHOOOOUUUSSSSEEEE!!

22 Oct 2020, 09:50

The Hells Bells doesn't like me riding a motorbike.
She calls it the effin bike, but not in a cute, cuddly way.
She framed the wee letter from the DVLNI to say it had been
scrapped, but not in a sympathetic, we will always remember it
way.
She kept telling me I was going to fall off it, and die, and orphan the
kids, and if I was to come home dead she would feckin kill me.

But then lockdown happened.
We were both stuck at home.
Together.
Alone.
With no buffer.
And no breaks.
Things changed.

Long Way Up was advertised.
On Apple TV, on Apple devices.
2 lads riding motorbikes up South America.

Not her sort of thing.
I said I would like to watch it, but I don't have an Apple product to watch Apple TV.
To my surprise she agreed about watching it.
And she set up a subscription.
Then she tried to screen share from her phone to the TV
That didn't work, sadly.
So she then gave me her actual phone.
But I told her it lasted hours and hours.
That wouldn't work either.
So she set it up on the Firestick.
And I am happily watching it.

So to clarify.

Pre lockdown, no motorbikes, you might get killed.

Post lockdown, here pet watch this interesting and intriguing documentary about motorbikes, and I don't mind if you start thinking and dreaming about motorbikes that might kill you.......

Hmmmm.

25 Oct 2020, 21:25

I was having a few pints in a pub once, and the PGA tour golf was on the TV. We were half yarning and half watching. There was a lad slouched at the corner of the bar who didn't like Rory. He claimed that there were at least 10 amateurs in Ireland who would have won more than Rory had they been given the same opportunities as Rory had. He quoted as proof one round of golf Rory played in Baltray when he was aged 14 and scored 80. Rory is totally overrated apparently, and its only media talk and people cheating that keeps him where he is.

Total utter complete ridiculous bullshit.

But nobody bothered to argue or debate with him. They ignored him. Total utter complete refusal to notice. He took that as confirmation that he was winning the argument, and continued to press home his imaginary advantage. He slouched in the corner, slurring his speech, looking at his pint, talking total utter and complete bullshit, and he was totally utterly and completely ignored by everyone there.

It reminded me of Trumps news conference last night.

In Irish pubs a clown like that gets ignored, and given another pint. In America he gets elected President, and given the nuclear codes.

Ah well.

6 Nov 2020, 09:55

Bye bye Trump.
Bye bye labelling immigrants as rapists and drug dealers.
Bye bye walls.
Bye bye college cheat, while accusing others.
Bye bye running from the draft. 5 times.
Bye bye labelling soldiers who suffered as losers, and criticising and lying about bereaved parents.
Bye bye justifying two white men beating up and pissing on a homeless immigrant.
Bye bye judging women on appearance, body shaming, calling them bimbos and devils and nasty, leaking blood, wanting them on their knees, grabbing them by the pussy, paying porn stars, and lusting over your daughter.
Bye bye lies about Obama birthplace.

Bye bye blaming Bush for 911.
Bye bye for falsely claiming Muslims in America celebrated 911.
Bye bye mocking the disabled.
Bye bye attempting to ban all Muslims.
Bye bye calling Iowa stupid.
Bye bye calling a rival a sex offender, another pussy, insulting another's wife, and accusing another's father of killing JFK.
Bye bye calling for violence against blacks, and offering to defend supporters charges with violence against blacks.
Bye bye threatening to actively target civilians in war.
Bye bye denying climate change, while your country is on fire.
Bye bye Putins puppet.
Bye bye gun lobby puppet.
Bye bye boasting of shooting people.
Bye bye lying about charity donations and crime statistics.
Bye bye business bankruptcy. 6 times.
Bye bye lying about your tax affairs while paying more tax in China than the USA.
Bye bye to justifying the KKK, neo Nazis and militant white supremacy groups.
Bye bye bragging about the size of your dick.
Bye bye censorship.
Bye bye tear gassing people for a photo opportunity.
Bye bye lying that an attack on Orlando happened in Atlanta. 3 times.
Bye bye to your truly horrible family.
Bye bye impeachment.
Bye bye 3 word chants.
Bye bye lying about Brexit.
Bye bye tax cuts which benefit your businesses.
Bye bye for lying about the Iraq war.
Bye bye praising Saddam. And Kim Jong Un. And Putin. And quoting Mussolini. And Russian hackers.
Bye bye claiming the primaries were rigged. And the democrat primaries were rigged. And the debates were rigged. And the presidential election was rigged. And the vote counting was rigged.

Bye bye visiting your election team in prison.
Bye bye claims that Obama founded ISIS.
Bye bye trying to fire nuclear weapons at hurricanes.
Bye bye separating migrant parents and children.
Bye bye sexual assault claims.
Bye bye letting hundreds of thousands die while you lied about Covid.
Bye bye trying to inject bleach to cure Covid.
Bye bye lying about your wealth.
Bye bye lying about your country's economics.
Bye bye claiming Swedish descent instead of German.
Bye bye insecurely lying about your inauguration crowd.
Bye bye to the winner of lie of the year 2015.
And 2017.
And 2019.
Fingers crossed for 2020.

7 Nov 2020, 19:03

I miss people. I always liked dogs, but liking people was a surprise to me. Not quite as much as I like dogs, but getting there.

I miss the way the most unexpected quiet people surprise me and astound me the most, and the loudest people surprise me the least. I'm left with social media where we tend to see those who shout the loudest. Cowardly dogs bark loudest.

I miss friends and relations, and their families and their little lives. I miss the way a child stumbles and goes to mammy for a bandage while trying not to cry and I smile sadly because my kids are grown up now, and then my child stumbles and comes in for a bandage while trying not to cry and I smile sadly and say feck off you are 22 now.

I miss BBQs on the decking that start with Budweiser and burgers and finish with Rockshore to sober up, but have had a bottle of red wine and a few gins in between, and they were the quiet nights. We are now having really quiet nights in.

I miss giving the kids the remote and letting them pick the weirdest videos on the digital TV.

I miss sunsets, I know they are still there, but they aren't the same. I don't bother much with sunrises.

I miss cafes and restaurants, sausages beans and toast taste nicer out. I miss listening and judging and noseying and interacting and not interacting, I miss the option.

I miss saying Grand Thanks when asked if everything is ok with a cold, burned meal that was served by a rude server. I miss not complaining. How was your complaining? Grand Tthanks

I miss the rain. I'm at home all the time, I haven't been caught in the rain in months. I wore my raincoat in the shower last week but it wasn't the same.

I miss the way at the end of every sentence the locals ask do you know what I mean? And if you agree they ask, But do you? Do you know what I mean? But do you?

I miss the tourists who went to Russia and took a flight in an Antonov plane that went up and down to simulate weightlessness, and I can do the same for free at the seven sisters in Gleno. I miss the tourists who think the white thing at the top of Croagh Patrick is a chippy van that a stag party from Dublin left there, and now we can't find the keys to bring it down. To be fair they think that because I told them that. I miss those tourists who spread joy when they arrive, and even more when they leave. I miss them.

I miss going to Tesco for a loaf, and coming back with a socket set, printer paper, a shirt, a digital radio, and some socks. But no bread.

I miss clients coming in for a 10-minute appointment and me keeping them hours chatting and drinking tay, and then finding out that they have left Mammy in the car.

I miss handshakes and hugs, didn't think I would but there you go.

I miss passing a building site and the wife saying Jaysus they threw that up.

I miss sport. It's not the same without the crowd. It's just not.

I miss pubs. Not nightclubs, but proper pubs with a fire in the corner and fish and chips on the menu. Pubs suit me. Nightclubs suit people who shout a lot and don't feel the need to listen. Nightclubs suit Dubs. I suit pubs.

I miss singsongs. Even the Christian ones. Possibly even the loyalist ones.

I miss silly people, impulsive people, interesting people, quirky people, odd people, surreal people. There are millions and millions of them in the world, and I've only met 627 according the Facebook. 628 if I count myself.

I miss standing when I'm sitting, and sitting when I'm standing.

I miss cycling. Moving. Travelling. Holidays. Chatting to strangers. Listening to strangers. Sharing with strangers. I know I can still do it, but it's not the same.

I miss having a haircut and someone else sweeping up. I have a lot of hair, and it spreads surprisingly far during cutting.

I miss meeting new people. I haven't met anyone new in months. I like new people that I haven't annoyed. Yet.

I miss breaking the seal.

I miss structure. But I miss the lack of structure too. I miss going for a walk up Cave hill or Divis or Donard just because I was there and so were they. Now I have to plan it. I don't like planning.

I miss walking slowly with my head up and listening to everyone and everything passing. I miss wondering why people walk with headphones on, diluting the experience.

I miss trying to judge drinking enough to get merry but not so much to get sick in the taxi home. Distance and road quality is always a factor. I miss getting the life stories from the taxi driver because they think I am so drunk I will never remember, but I do. I do. Or at least I think I do. Maybe I don't.

I miss remembering things that never happened at all. It's all true, and some of it actually happened.

I miss not having to find an excuse not to go to the gym. I've come up with a couple of absolute crackers lately, but they have been wasted. Such a shame. And when the gyms reopen, I will have run out of excuses. Such a shame.

I miss the rivalry between Ford and Chevy in the States, Ford and Holden in Oz, and Ford and Massey in Ireland.

I miss Slimming World and the way they would look at me. That was a surprise to me. To them I'm the ultimate bad boy with hope of redemption. It's nice to be the bad boy sometimes.

I miss walking more than 800 steps a day. My Fitbit is in single figures.

I miss telling people that I work from home on a Monday Wednesday Friday, and I live at the office on a Tuesday and Thursday and Saturday. It's all the same thing now.

I miss sneaking out for breakfast with the HB on a Saturday morning and worrying if the waitress would ask if I wanted the usual.

I miss Friday night date night with herself. I miss Monday night date night with the lads.

I miss baby Guinness and flaming sambucas. But never the other way round.

I miss tractors. I haven't seen a tractor since March. Have tractors all succumbed to the virus? Have you seen a tractor? Well? Have you?

I miss grounding kids. They are already grounded. So am I. We all are. No point grounding them anymore.

I miss asking for the sweet menu. Our sweet menu at home is a Pearpickingporkie or a fish finger.

I miss not going to mass. Yes, you read that right. In a couple of weeks we have tickets for mass. Allocated seating. Think we got them on ticket master. Presale. We have to go, or we will be missed. And I will have to put a note into the collection plate. Reduced congregation, a coin just won't do, hell would beckon. Now, what comes after consubstantial with?

I miss fate and accident and chance. Things now feel stale and sterile.

I miss the way we cheer the disasters and commiserate with the successes when we should do it the other way round.

I miss opportunities.

I miss laughing at conspiracy theorists because if we all go back to work they have won, and if we all stay in lockdown they have won. Covid has empowered the eejits.

But you know something?
When all is said and done?
You know what i find?
The tougher things get?
The stronger our resolve becomes.

Anyway morning all.
No mass today.
Couldn't get tickets.

15 Nov 2020, 10:36

I know I've loads of VAT.
And a lot of PAYE.
And 2 CIS queries.
And quite a few sets of accounts, some of which are urgent.
And I'm missing my wee worker daughter, who has moved on to pastures new and bigger and better.

But I'm lucky.
I have supportive and understanding clients.
They know the score.

So right now I am at the top of a mountain. It's perfect. The wind was at my back coming uphill so it pushed me up, and in my face coming down the hill so it stopped me falling forward. Perfect. Everyone is nodding hello and in good form and glad to be out while

keeping their distance. Perfect.
Lots of people are in boots and waterproof trousers, Gore-Tex coats and rucksacks. I'm in shifting shoes, dress trousers, TGI Fridays shirt, and golf jacket. Perfect.
The rain threatened but didn't come even though I had my brolly. Perfect.
The temperature is cold when I stop walking, and cool when I am walking. Perfect.
And the day is overcast but I can still see Belfast. Perfect.
I'm taking this one hour off to go walking. Perfect.

And this afternoon and evening?
Every bit of work will be done, ready for tomorrow's emergency. Perfect.

16 Nov 2020, 15:06

I was cooking. Chicken curry, rice and chips.

I decided to try make it a bit special.
I decided to try present it nicely.
I decided to try make an effort.

So I spooned the rice carefully exactly in the centre of her plate, and smoothed it down level and round and not a grain out of place. Lovely.
On my plate I just dumped what was left, including crusty bits from the bottom of the pan, just on the side of my plate.

Then I placed the nicest looking chips delicately on her plate round the outside so they were just touching the edge of the rice without mixing, and numbered them so they were evenly spread and equally distant from the edge. Lovely
On my plate I just dumped what was left half on and half off the

rice, half on and half off the plate. I scraped up the chips that had missed the plate. 5 second rule.

I then delicately placed the finest, most even chunks of chicken and the nicest peppers right in the middle of the rice surrounded by chips and carefully spooned just the right amount of curry sauce on the chicken taking great care not to drip sauce on the edge of the plate. Lovely.
On my plate I slopped and scraped and dumped the rest of the crud from the pan onto the pile of rice and chips.

And I called her in, while I stood with a tea towel folded over my arm like a proper waiter, and waited to be appreciated.

She walked in, looked at the two plates, thanked me, lifted mine, and off she went.

Ah well.
Serves me right.
Pretentious prat.
16 Nov 2020, 19:56

Some days you just bounce out of bed, and sing loud and proud in the shower and you just know it's going to be a good day. And it will.

Other days you might have to tell yourself to get up and might have to tell yourself to sing in the shower and might have to tell yourself you can have a good day. And maybe you will.

Finally occasionally you need to have a duvet day and stay in the PJs eat chocolate and drink wine and look after yourself and just reset. And that's OK too. As long as you make yourself sing in the shower the next morning.

Morning all. Did you hear me singing this morning?? Loud and proud lads, loud and proud.

18 Nov 2020, 09:40

I'm a celeb.
High enjoyable.
Great fun.
Brings back memories for me.

Rank, rotten food causing nausea, in a big cold draughty castle.

It reminds me of the day we took the kids to that Tayto place in Tandragee.

Nite all.

18 Nov 2020, 22:25

Called to a client in Stranmillis.
Free parking space right outside.
That was handy.
Went in and had a bit of craic with the client and the customers.
That was lovely.
Came out and saw a wee coffee shop next door, takeaway only, so I went over and ordered a hot chocolate for a cold day.
Lovely.

Two sisters were also waiting.
Late 30s, early 40s.
Seemed like nice likeable people.

We waited.
We yarned.
While distancing.
They liked my clicky shoes, I liked their posh Malone Road accents.
It was just lovely, and a wee touch of normality.

Nice car, sister one says.
They looked at each other.
Sister two nodded her agreement.

Thanks says me.

Tell me, sister two says, is there a Missus nice car?
They looked at each other.
Sister one nodded her agreement.

Well!!
Here is a turnup for the books.
Still got it big man.
Still got it.
I tucked my tummy in.
I hoiked my trousers up.
Put a sympathetic face on.
There is says me proudly.
The Hells Bells says me.
28 years now says me.

That's a pity, sister one says
Yeah, sister two says resignedly.
Yeah, sister one agreed sadly.
We are on the lookout for a man, sister two explained.
For our mammy, sister one clarified.

Bubble burst.
Ah well.
Another wee touch of normality there........

It's tough times.
It's been a shitty week.
For all of us.

But this week I found a few things out. About wee local lovely people doing wee local lovely things.

Against regulations, a post man who delivers the post locally will collect a letter or letters or cards and post them for people that struggle to get out. Good on him.

Against regulations, certain bin men in East Belfast have been walking down the side of a house, opening the gate, down 2 steps, collecting a bin, emptying the bin, and leaving it back to where it was to help an elderly couple that struggle to get out. Good on them.

Against regulations, some bin men here will empty bins, and take stuff at the side of the house that isn't in the bin to save elderly people having to order a special pick up or a skip. Good on them.

Some Taxi drivers will take vulnerable people to the doctors, then go visit someone who apparently lives close by, and wait and take the people home while only charging them a fare one way. Good on them.

There are dozens and dozens of little things being done by local people for local people to help each other get through. And I think that's just class.

Evening all.
If we can winter this one out, we can summer anywhere.

Take care, see you in the morning x

22 Nov 2020, 22:12

I don't care how old and tired and stressed and under pressure you are, but when the Balance Sheet total comes out at £53,180.08 you giggle. Like a child. Repeatedly.

0.7734 all. If you don't know what I'm on about, 376006 it. Let me know if you remember your school days and this makes you 376616 too.

30 Nov 2020, 11:38

LIVE YOUR LIFE.

If we have learned anything this week, it's that we need to live our lives. Things could change drastically next week, or next month, or next year.

Stop trying to impress people, impress yourself. Impress your family. Impress your friends.

The most brilliant people in some ways are often the weakest in others. Enjoy your brilliance, but work at it. Accept your limitations, but work on them too.

Never berate yourself. And don't let other people to berate you either. Their opinion of you is none of your business. Tell them that. Explain that to them. Don't tell them that your affairs are none of THEIR business, tell them that THEIR opinion of your affairs is none of YOUR business. That confuses them.

Walk away from people who make you feel bad. And don't berate yourself for it. Life is too short. Life is too special.

Your competition isn't other people, it isn't family, it isn't friends, it isn't workmates, its yourself. Make yourself the best yourself you can be. Look at your expectations for yourself, and try to match them. Praise your successes, work on your shortcomings.

Help people. Helping people helps you too. Keep doing it right up until the very minute helping people doesn't help you. Once you stop getting the positive buzz from helping people, it's time to reduce your involvement. And don't berate yourself for stepping away.

Some people don't want helped, they want enabled. Learn the difference. Helping is good. Enabling is bad.

Only sad people insist that the customer is always right. The rest of us know that the customer is seldom wrong. There is a difference.

You will make mistakes. Apologise if need be and move on.
People will make mistakes. Let them apologise if need be and move on.
Spitefulness and nastiness are not mistakes, they are character traits. Cut them out if you find them in yourself. Tell other people to cut it out if you find it in them. Never berate yourself for this.

Eyebrows are facial hair too.

Reflect.
Consider.
Stupid people don't reflect or consider, that's why they are always so certain. And so regularly wrong.

Where ignorance is bliss, sometimes it's foolish to be wise.

Advise people if they ask for it, don't advise them if they don't. Accept people's advice as a general guide, but not as a bible. Be adventurous that way. You know what's best for you. You always know best.

Share your opinion, and allow others to share theirs. Feel free to ignore theirs, and don't get annoyed if they ignore yours. Remember, a difference of opinion is not a reason to fall out, however, not being allowed to have or to express an opinion is a good reason.

Fight for what you believe in, and don't ever let anyone speak down to you.

You can't work on your mental health when you are struggling, you will need to focus on just getting thorough the day. The time to work on it is NOW. Same with physical health. Go take a walk.

Compliment other people, allow them to compliment you. Don't insult anyone, unless they insult you. And remember that a patronising smile can be the biggest insult there is. Remember the complements, ignore the insults. Both ways.

Never cook on a high heat. Except for steak. For everything else, take your time.

Refuse to rush. Refusing to rush is a great way to go.

A smile improves everything.

Social Media isn't real life. Its highlights. And lowlights. That's all. Don't trust it, don't believe it, don't rely on it, don't make any decisions based on it. It's not real.

Don't shape fact to suit your opinion, shape your opinion to suit facts.

You can push people a little bit, or you can lead them for miles and miles. Your choice.

Misery loves company. Don't get dragged there.

You are not too fat,
you are not too tall,
you are not too skinny,
you are not too small,
You are you.
And if you are reading this you are on my friends list.
And if you are on my friends list it's because you have done something to impress me.
No other reason.
So well done to you.

And one last thing to remember.

Just because I've told you something doesn't make it true.

Evening all.
Stay safe. x

4 Dec 2020, 17:03

I don't care how slippery it is.
I don't care how icy it is.
I don't care how fast I'm going on the bike.
I don't care how slow they are going walking.
I don't care how narrow the path is.
I don't care how many pedestrians are about.

I don't care about the carnage that would ensue if I was to clatter into them at speed.
I don't care about Covid 19, 20 or even 21.

When a little lad with Down Syndrome holds out his hand as you are haring and tearing and sliding on the bike down the path towards him, you hold out your hand too.
When you see him ignoring Dads slightly exasperated but shurewhatcanyoudo face, you ignore it too.
When you see the little lads very excited face you get a very excited face too.
When you hear the little lads big cheer as you high five, you give back a big cheer too.
When you think maybe that made the little lads day just got a tiny touch brighter, you realise the little lad just made your day a huge big massive unbelievable touch brighter.

Afternoon all.

Isn't life grand?

PS.

I don't know who they were, but maybe you do. If you happen to know of a family that would have been on the Lisburn side of Shaws Bridge about noon today, please tell them that the little lad with the huge smile made my day. Thanks.

6 Dec 2020, 13:30

So anyway.

I sat last night watching Virgin River, which doesn't feature virgins and only the merest glance of a river. Picture the lovechild of Grays

Anatomy and Ballykissangel, dialogue written by Hallmark Cards. And I was drinking tea that was far too milky from a cup that the finger hole was far too small, but I had made the tea myself and picked the cup myself, so all wounds were self-inflicted. Sado masochism without the sado part.
And I was nibbling a Rich Tea and trying to pretend it was a Digestive. Mental torture.
And I was out of proper Tayto, while the Yellow pack mob have dropped their prices to 9.475 pence per bag (VAT incl), I was listening to the Nordies somehow still claim they are a premium product and while they were at it that Cookstown slice their rashers thick. Even Trump would have conceded long ago. 9.475 pence per bag. Jaysus. Still too dear.
And I was wondering where my masculinity had gone.

Anyway.

Despite all.

I'm still posting, you are still reading, I'm still seeing the funny side, the Hells Bells is still being the Hells Bells, and Mel and Jack finally shifted in Virgin River at the end of episode 8. Or maybe 9. Then they fell out in 10.
Things could be worse, couldn't they?
Can't wait for season 2.

9 Dec 2020, 11:02

I had a masked, socially distanced meeting with a client. She is mid-20s, has a nice business, lives in a nice apartment, drives a nice car, and takes her wee mummy with her everywhere. She is a very impressive and likeable character.

She saw some Cycle Against Suicide stuff in the office, she asked, I told her about promoting mental health in schools and clubs. She then started to tell me her experience.

She suffered and suffers from depression, poor mental health, and self-harm, and now she is living in one of the finest apartments in Belfast, and driving a very nice and completely impractical car.

She left school as soon as she possibly could with a C in Art and a C in Home Economics, and yet now she is running her own very successful business.

Her wee mummy says she was badly bullied at school, but the daughter reckons she just didn't fit in, and now she employs her biggest tormentor at school in her factory. She doesn't do it to show a bully who is boss, but to give a person a chance. Plus, she is the best person for the job.

She suffers from dyslexia, couldn't and still can't do basic maths, so now she employs the smartest girl in the class as her bookkeeper. Not to show a teacher's pet who is the boss, but because she is the best person for the job.

No boyfriend, no girlfriend, she isn't just ready yet.

Her wee mummy reckons the kids at school were cruel, but daughter reckons they were merciless. The daughter volunteers at the weekend in a soup kitchen to give something back and show some mercy herself.

Oh and see the way she takes Mummy everywhere?
It's because despite all she has achieved and all she has beaten, she doesn't have the confidence to have a meeting without her Mummy by her side.

Despite all, she has a wonderful knack of making life simple. If only she knew it.

The bigger the obstacles, the higher she climbs.

Nite all x.

10 Dec 2020, 21:37

Little things matter.

6 weeks ago.
Felt tired.
Felt exhausted.
Felt shattered.
Felt sore.
Working too hard.
Doing too many hours.
No walking.
Needed a holiday.
Eating bad food.
At bad times.
Not seeing friends.
Not seeing family.
Not getting fresh air.
Just felt shite.

Needed to make a change.

So I did.
A big change for me, but a tiny change for some.

I started taking multivitamins. Religiously.
They give me fluorescent sparkly pee, a wee boost in energy, and a wee drop in fatigue.
And because I had a wee boost in energy, I got my work done a wee

bit quicker.
And because i was getting my work done a wee bit quicker I was able to get out for a regular walk and an occasional cycle.
And because I was out walking and cycling I was sleeping better.
And because I was sleeping better, I wasn't jaded all day.
And because I wasn't jaded all day I was able to get rid of the bad food at the bad times and plan a bit better.
And because I'm planning a bit better everything seems a bit more under control and a bit less pressured.
And the fluorescent pee is a colourful quirky wee rainbow filled bonus.

Try it. If you need to. Or if you want to.
Make a wee change.
Just one wee change.
And then sit back, and watch things improve.

Amazing how much little things matter.

Evening all.

Isn't life grand?

13 Dec 2020, 21:41

I was stopped at the lights at the bottom of Greenisland on a cold damp Belfast morning.
Me and John Farnham.
Him singing with tone and talent, me singing along with enthusiasm and gusto.

A Land Rover pulled into the land beside me.
A big white armoured Landie.
And it bouncing.

Because the lads in the front and presumably the back were also singing along.
And Dad dancing.

So we had a wee sing along together, while we waited for the lights to change.

Nice moment.

Morning all.
Sing with gusto today.
Give her pepper today lads, give her pepper......

14 Dec 2020, 10:01

I was force-fed advice from some intense people who are adamant that they aren't going to take the vaccine they haven't been offered yet because they aren't sure it's safe and don't know what's in it.

However from enquiries made, I seem to recall that one is a lady who takes steroids (she calls them supplements) from a lad who claims to be Linford Christine's former supplier, another gets Botox in the Shankill in an upstairs bedroom from a girl she saw on Facebook, and got tattoos in Benidorm at a pop up Tattoo stand that stored needles in a jam jar, while the fellow giving advice eats Cookstown ham family pack 16 slices for two quid with minimum 18.9% meat every day as part of his keto diet.

Ok then.
I didn't argue.
It all seems fair enough.
It wasn't a debate, it was more of a lecture.
I didn't, wouldn't, and couldn't point out any flaw in their

intentions, nor question their lack of expertise.
However I do think I would be worried about that ham.

15 Dec 2020, 10:23

Talking to a local lad.
One of these lucky lads that has a deep and varied expert knowledge on a wide range of issues both at home and abroad gained from his vast experience surviving on sick benefit and delivering takeaway food every night in his DLA car.

He told me how lucky I was to be here, and to be given a free car as an immigrant and a free house as a Roman Catholic.
He honestly believed all this.
Common knowledge in Ballymena apparently.
All the immigrants get free cars apparently.
And the Catholic Church gives all Roman Catholics free houses to address the population imbalance in Ulster and reassert Rome rule apparently.
Also common knowledge in Ballymena.
Apparently.

I started to put him straight, but he was having none of it.
He was adamant.
Common knowledge in Ballymena apparently.

So I decided to have some fun.

They don't give us a house, says me.
Nooo, says me.
But I will tell you what they do do, says me.
His eyes and ears pricked up.

I started to giggle at the sheer ridiculousness of it all.

Do do, says me.
I said do do, says me giggling, to cover up my giggles.
They give you a grant for 50%, says me, and guarantee a mortgage for the rest, says me.
No questions asked, says me.
So the do do, I giggled.

And I did a nod and a wink.

I knew it, he declared, adamantly.
He had been vindicated.

But do you know what annoys me most, says me?
What, he asked?
Converts get a 90% grant, I declared.
Do they he asked?
Yep, I declared.
If a man and his family convert from Protestantism to Catholicism, they get a 90% grant to buy a house, I claimed.
Up to a max of 300 grand, I sputtered!!
I don't think that's fair I declared.
90% I declared!!!
Everyone should get the same, I declared!!!

He was in a quandary.
He agreed that it was completely totally and utterly wrong when the other ones were getting preferential treatment, but wasn't so sure it was wrong when preferential treatment was available to him and his ones.
He was adding it up.
90% grant of 300 grand for a house. 270k.

He wanted to know how that worked.

Go see the priest, says me.
Tell him you want to convert, says me.

Give him the nod and the wink, says me.
He will understand, says me.
Get you and the family baptised, says me.
Get the kids to make their first holy communion, says me.
Takes about a year, says me.
And then get them to collect the communion money, says me.
You have heard the phrase communion money, says me?
He had.
That's what it relates to, says me.
He didn't know that.
He thought it was the money collected from the relatives.
Ahhh no, says me.
That's what they want you to think, says me.
Hiding in plain sight, says me.

And I gave the wink and the nod.
He gave it back.

Anyway.
I better go to confession.
I have a feeling I have just sinned.
And also I have a feeling that the priest might need to be prepared
for a visitor........

Common knowledge in Ballymena apparently.

21 Dec 2020, 14:05

Went to Bridge Street Belfast to pick up the post.
Nowhere to park, except the taxi rank.
Big queues into the car parks.
No warden go be seen.
It will be grand.
2 mins.

Its Christmas.
Do well.

Popped it in the taxi rank, ran to the office, grabbed the post,
Happy Christmas and all that, ran back out, right behind a traffic
warden.
He was excited.
I could tell.
Maybe he was one victim away from his Christmas bonus.
He was marching.
He was striding.
He was stridently striding.
Down towards my car.

I followed him.
He walked straight down the footpath, eyes on the prize, I headed
right and walked down the road.
I struggled to keep up, that's how fast he was going.
He strode down the length my car at speed, got out his wee pad
thing, and stepped out at the front of the car to check the number
plate.
I blipped the door.
He saw the lights flash and did an about turn.
He checked behind him.
Rookie mistake.
I was actually right in front of him.
I reached the door and opened it.

He can't give me a ticket if I'm in the car.
He turned back and saw me.
He wasn't happy.
He wasn't happy at all.
Christmas bonus disappearing.
He strode over to me.
I kept the open door between us.

Let the games commence.

You cannae park here, he growled.

Touch aggressive there sunshine.
No real call for that.
I decided to be polite in reply.

Would you mind stepping back please, says me?
Social distancing and all that, says me?
2 metres, says me?
Thank you sir, says me.

He took a token step back. Maybe a foot. Maybe not.

I have te gie ye a ticket, he growled again.

I was still exceedingly polite.

Again sir, I says.
I'm not having this conversation while you are inside 2 metres, I
explained.
I apologise but I have vulnerable people in my care and I'm not
prepared to take the risk, says me.
Social distancing, says me.
Back beside the headlight would be fine, says me.
Thank you very much sir, I appreciate this, says me.

A crowd was watching.
He had to comply.
He went back beside the headlight.

You're parked illegally and I have to gie ye a ticket he declared.

I got into the car.
Sorry mate, I called out.
I started the car.

Can't hear ye, I yelled.
I closed the door.
Happy Christmas, I roared.

And I drove off round him much to the enjoyment of the passers-by.

Morning all.
Isn't life just grand??
Tough yeah.
But still grand??

Happy Christmas lads.

23 Dec 2020, 11:58

Anyway.
I'm 50 early next year, and there is such a thing as 50 things to do before you are 50. I'm a bit late to the party, so I'm going to do 50 something things to do while I'm in my 50 something.
However.
Some of them are done, so I may need some quirky replacements. You lot know me by now. Feel free to make suggestions.

1. Crack an egg one handed. I've always admired the way chefs do this, but I just can't master it. Not consistently. Now, you may think I'm starting small, but with my hand eye coordination and lack of delicate touch, this one is tricky.

2. Hoover the house top to bottom. This was suggested by the Hells Bells, and she had a right wee chuckle at her cleverness. So she did.

3. Get Chinese takeaway papers back in the bag as neat as they came out. I've never done it. Most of the time I can't even open the

knot they put in the top of the bag. Have you done this? Honestly?

4. Cycle through a car wash, pay my 4 quid and get a power wash and a polish.

5. Ask what the soup of the day is, then take the soup.

6. Drive a car round Silverstone. DONE. REPLACEMENT NEEDED.

7. Write a book. DONE. REPLACEMENT NEEDED.

8. Go round the Isle of Man track on 2 wheels. Motorbike, bike, or sideways in a car.

9. Put fairy liquid in a fountain. I wonder how many bottles I would need to create a foamy paradise?

10. March in an Orange march to see what it's all about. I sort of planned it this year but the marches were cancelled. I was only an Orange man for a few weeks, and already I'm sick of all the feckin rerouting.

11. Swim the piers in Carlingford. Did this years ago, want to do it again

12. Juggle 3 things.

13. Eat Frogs legs and Escargot.

14. Go to the funeral for someone who donated their body to medical science.

15. Cheese rolling in Gloucester. Not sure about this one. REPLACEMENT NEEDED.

16. Meet the president. DONE. REPLACEMENT NEEDED.

17. Crash a wedding photo on a Jet ski. DONE. REPLACEMENT NEEDED.

18. Land a ball on the 9th green in Lough Erne from 120 yards away on the boat doing 20 knots. Harder than you think.

19. Visit Malin and Mizen. Never done either.

20. Go Heli skiing. No idea what it is, but it sounds good, doesn't it? It will be nice to involve the Hells Bells too.

21. Do a stand-up comedy gig.

22. Fire walk.

23. See Grand Canyon. DONE. REPLACEMENT NEEDED.

24. Cycle the Golden Gate. DONE. REPLACEMENT NEEDED.

25. Drive 155mph on the Autobahn. I tried it on the M1 heading north after the toll at Drogheda, but chickened out at 140.

26. Ask a midget if he is Santa's little helper. DONE. REPLACEMENT NEEDED.

27. Fix the sign in Fermanagh. There is a sign just past Ballygawley Roundabout that says Augher, Clogher, Enniskillen. That's wrong. You can't have Augher, Clogher without adding Fivemiletown. It grates with me.

38. Chase the bulls in Pamplona. I'm not big on running away.

39. Visit Skellig Micheal but ignore the Star Wars shite. This may not be possible.

40. Cycle from the Irish Sea to the Atlantic Ocean in one day. Or vice versa. Salt water to salt water.

41. Use the guest towels in someone else's house, or see a guest in our house use our guest towels.

42. See the booby mating dance in Galapagos (I just like the sound of this)

43. Sumo wrestle in a real sumo contest.

44. Get a tattoo.

45. Do an eating challenge. It may be best to schedule this soon before any cycling/hiking challenges.

46. Walk the Camino. Portuguese Camino, 1 week. Covid scuppered this year's plans.

47. Go through the Chanel Tunnel. That's if it's still open after Brexit.

48. Get a letter published on Dear Deirdre. I can't count the number of letters I've written, but with no luck.

49. Cycle Carrickfergus to Fermanagh.

50. Climb Donard DONE, Carrantouhill, Lugnaquilla, and Croagh Patrick. And try at least one of Snowdon, Scafell and Ben Nevis.

51. Learn to be as good with the ladies as George Micheal or as macho as Freddie Mercury. Legends. May not be possible.

52. Put all the dishes in the dishwasher without needing to be corrected.

53. Learn to play the ukulele. Or guitar. Or any instrument.

54. Walk from Asia to Europe.

55. F1 weekend.

56. See the northern lights. DONE. REPLACEMENT NEEDED.

57. Write an app.

58. Sail Carrick to Portpatrick. And back.

59. McDonald's Drive through. In a Massey 565 mainly because the door is on the wrong side. Or a 575 585 or 595, I'm not fussy.

60. Cycle Dublin to Belfast. Or Belfast to Dublin.

This is a wish list, apart from that bloody sign. That sign is a necessity.

29 Dec 2020, 12:24

Come on, let's go out for breakfast love.

Whatever you want pet.

Maxol, BP or Texaco.....

31 Dec 2020, 11:06

I miss me kids, one in England, the other just up the road.
I miss me Mammy and me Daddy.

I miss me brudders and me sister and me nephews and me nieces and the rest of the clan.
I miss me mates.
I miss me golf.
I miss Fermanagh.
I miss Mr Tayto.
It's been a shite year.

But we will all see each other soon.

So I'm actually grateful.

I'm grateful to everyone that wore a mask.
And to everyone that disinfected.
And to everyone that isolated.
And to everyone that did the best they could possibly do to stop this pandemic reaching so many more people.
And to the nurses and the doctors that saved thousands upon thousands of lives.
And to the teachers and shop workers and hauliers and all the people who went out when we stayed in.
And to the Zoom quizzers, and the Facebook live singers, and to the doorstep clappers, and to the dreamers and the writers for keeping us going.
And to everyone that tried.

That's why I'm grateful.

See you all next year.
Take care lads.

31 Dec 2020, 23:29

The way new year works.

New Year's Eve. Right big lad, new year new you. Drinking water, eating better, doing sit-ups, walking, cycling. Here we go!!!

New Year's day. Tired, hungover, late night, fridge full of food, waste not want not, poor starving kids in Tallaght and all that, shure we can't throw it out. Start tomorrow. Here we go!!!

2nd January. Its Saturday. Shite. Forgot about that. Saturday is Party day. Can't start on Saturday. No-one ever started anything on a Saturday. Except a sesh. Start tomorrow. Here we go!!!

3rd January. Its Sunday. Can't start on Sunday. It's illegal, illegitimate and immoral to start anything on a Sunday. Start Monday. Here we go!!!

4th January. Might as well wait until the next new year now.......

2 Jan 2021, 17:06

Monday morning.

I managed to tear the packet of Weetabix and spill crumbs all over the counter and the floor. I cleaned the counter, but left the floor, no one will notice a few crumbs.
I then managed to then dribble milk over the counter I had just cleaned while pouring it into the pan to heat. I wiped that up while the milk was heating.
I then managed to dribble the warm milk while pouring it onto the Weetabix onto the counter i had just cleaned twice. So, I cleaned it. Again.
I then managed to pour sweetener out of the non-perforated side of the jar, and ended up with about 18 spoons of sweetener in the

bowl. However, I viewed it as an improvement, because I didn't have to clean the counter.

And now I'm going to do some lucky clients accountancy work.

Update. The Hells Bells just went into the kitchen and she noticed. Of course, she did. The floor is crunchy. How could she not? There's Weetabix, milk and sweetener everywhere. Ah well.

Morning all. Isn't life grand??

4 Jan 2021, 10:43

I was feeling warm and a touch uncomfortable, I was just back from a walk, I had drunk a pint of water or two to cool down, but it wasn't working. I was light headed, the house was boiling, I decided I needed to turn the heat down before I passed out.

I went in to inform the HB.

She was in her office, and she was sitting wearing a fleece.
With a scarf.
And a blanket.
And a halogen heater at her feet.
And she still looked cold.

I decided to leave the heating alone. I went outside for a bit.

Everyone else is worried about COVID, I'm worried about Heatstroke, the HB is worried about Hypothermia. You couldn't make it up.

5 Jan 2021, 16:12

I was out for a stroll along Fisherman's Quay, and I wandered up behind a lad standing right in the middle of the pier scanning the horizon through his binoculars. He was scanning left to right, looking at Bangor and turning for Holywood then Belfast, I passed him on the left so as not to disturb him and wandered on.

I reached the end of the pier and kicked the wall (it's a Galway thing, you have to kick the wall when walking, don't ask me why, ask a Tribesman or Tribeswoman) and turned to come back. Binoculars man had scanned left to right through Holywood and Belfast and Carrick Castle and was now rotating right to left back towards me.

I thought I would be funny.

I waited 20 feet from him and put a gormless grin on my face and waited for his rotation to put my gormless face in his binocular eyeline. He would be startled, I would giggle, he would giggle, we would become socially distanced giggle buddies and have a wee tale to tell when we got home.

His rotation reached me.
He wasn't startled, he didn't giggle.
He was scared shitless.
He jumped, he jerked, he stumbled, he squealed.
And he glared at me.
And he swore at me.

Ah well.
In hindsight I'm not sure we were all that well suited as giggle buddies, it wouldn't have lasted. I don't have binoculars.

7 Jan 2021, 15:31

I've just realised something.

Many years ago a client and his son came to see me, the son had special needs, he was severely autistic, nonverbal, and didn't interact with anyone outside the immediate family. I didn't patronise the lad, I didn't speak down to him, I just told him to relax with the TV remote and have him the run of the house. Dad was concerned, but I wasn't. In return the son recorded Homes under the Hammer and an excellent Moon Landing documentary for me and deleted some stuff that he wasn't interested in, and then thanked me with a high five when he was leaving. Dad was amazed and delighted, and explained that he just doesn't interact with anyone else. I asked if people interact with him.

The following year he explored upstairs, played pool and darts and I was rewarded with eye contact. Son had relaxed. So had I. So had Dad. Dad was chuffed.

A couple of years later he took me by the arm and dragged me outside to show me the car parked in the drive. I went, even though I knew all about the car, after all it was my car. Dad was astounded.

In between they had visited once when he was having a bad day, so Dad made an excuse to come back again when he was having a better day. If lads can't won't or don't come into our lives, we can always try to go into theirs.

Last year Dad phoned me to come to the door, and him and his son and his puppy bounced down the lane in a tiny, old, battered wee car with L plates, son driving and bouncing and grinning the biggest grin I have ever seen, and Dad terrified and cowering and hanging on for dear life. I smiled, then chuckled, then roared laughing, then gurned at possibly the most wonderful, ridiculous sight I had ever seen.

This year I was really looking forward to their annual visit and update.

And that's what I've just realised.

It's not going to happen.

Ah well. There's always next year. Stay safe lads.

Ahhh women.
Gotta love the women.

What about that computer work she says?
Will we do that wee job now she says?
I'm ready she says.
I'm ready right now she says.
I have everything ready she says.
Come on she says.
Let's finish the wee job now she says.
When it's fresh in the mind she says.
And I have everything ready she says.
You will be proud of me she says.
Let's go she says.
Come on she says.

I conceded.

Ok says me, let's go.

She was delighted.

Ok she says

Just give me 20 minutes to get ready.......

Ahhh women. Gotta love the women.

9 Jan 2021, 20:47

Missed a call from a panicky client. He left a voicemail.

Big man, he said.
Call me back urgently, he gasped.
Please, he begged.
As soon as you possibly can, he implored.
Please, he pleaded.

I called him back as soon as I was free.
I was worried.
It wasn't like him to be panicky.
My call went straight to voicemail.
Was it the HMRC?
Had he been served a summons?
Was there tax collectors there?

I called again.
Straight to voicemail.

Or was it illness?
Oh God no.
Not the kids.
His kids are lovely.
And he is a single parent, and he dotes on his kids.
This is terrible.
Truly terrible.

I tried again.

It rang.
He answered.
Finally.
Phew.

Thanks be to God he gasped.
What's up says me?
We are desperate he declared.
What happened says me?
We are at our wits end he told me.
What's wrong says me?
We don't know where to turn he sobbed.
WHAT IS WRONG says me?

He took a deep breath. Clearly this was going to be rough.

Its fractions, he declared.
We are trying to add fractions, he declared.
How the feck do you add fractions, he begged.
Please, he begged.
You are our last hope, he pleaded.
Kids are in tears and me completely lost, he told me.
Please, he sobbed.

Oh crap. Fractions. It's worse than I thought.

13 Jan 2021, 21:48

I was going to the office yesterday to collect my post. The Hells Bells decided to join me.

She approved my route, and guided me on what lane I needed to be in, she selected where to park, she debated which of us was going in and which waiting in the car, and adjusted and approved my apparel before I finally went in.

I was glad of the help, after all I've only been going to that office alone for 17 years......

17 Jan 2021, 21:35

Well, that's it lads.
The most powerful man in the world is a Cooley culchie.

Bull bars and fake alloys on Air Force One.
She's chipped and running on red lads
A presidential John Deere 4wd ready for drawing hay.
Marty Mone or Nathan singing the anthem.
Quoting Father Ted. I'M NO GOOD AT JUDGING THE SIZE OF CROWDS TED, BUT I'D SAY THERE'S ABOUT SEVENTEEN MILLION OF THEM OUT THERE.
Child of Prague and JFK on the mantel.
Canada Dry Orange and Joker ice lollys.
Taking a hurl to his first meeting. An Puc Fada lads. Wearing a Kilkenny Jersey. Matched with Tyrone shorts. Up de cats lads....
Getting Hilary or Bill to touch the electric fence. Go on der boy.....
Twitter posts about customs dippin.
Cant have a meeting, he has to go to a wake. Ahh sorry for your loss.....
Yeeeeooooo, horse it into ya Kamala, you're the girl fer me......

Cant wait lads, can't wait.

20 Jan 2021, 18:08

Lockdown is starting to bite in the most unexpected ways.

We are painfully low on pint glasses, and all the pubs are closed.
How can we get more?
Can we buy pint glasses somewhere?
Do people ever buy pint glasses?
I never have?
Have you?
Presumably pubs do, but normal people?
I don't think so.

We need the pubs open, and we need them NOW!!!!

21 Jan 2021, 09:33

I started tidying up after the Chinese.
She looked at me with surprise

I scraped the scant remains of the boiled rice box into the remains
of the salt and chilli veg box, and put the empty boiled rice box
under the salt and chilli box nice and neat.
She looked at me impressed.

I scraped the dribble of remains of the onions and sauce from the
chicken curry on top of the rice and salt and chilli veg box, and put
the empty box underneath the boiled rice box nice and neat.
She looked at me admiringly.

I took the couple of chips that were left over out of the bag and put
them into the chicken curry salt and chilli veg rice box, and screwed
up the bag and put it in the bin nice and neat.
She looked at me with desire.

I mixed them all together and started to eat.

It was absolutely gorgeous.
A wee taste of Salt and Chilli Veg Curry
Chip with boiled rice.
She looked at me with disappointment.

Don't really know why.

What about all the starving kids in Rathcoole pet?
Would they not be glad of a wee salt and chilli mix pet?
Waste not, want not pet.
Yum xx

21 Jan 2021, 20:04

Morning all.

The wealthiest man is the one who needs the least to make him happy.

Have a good day.

22 Jan 2021, 08:56

I stopped to help a wee man holding on to the railing, he had dropped his stick.

Thanks son he says.
No bother says me.
Its slippery he says.
Tis says me.
And cold he says.
Tis says me.

I don't walk fast enough these days to get warm he says.
You're doing ok says me.
I walk two miles a day he says.
Good man says me.
I used to walk twenty two he says.
Did ya says me?
I did he says.
He smiled.
I smiled.
But then I had two good legs and I was courting when I got home he says.
Fair play to ya says me.
Now I've only one good leg and a limp and not a court in years he says.
I laughed.

Sounds like most of us are in the same boat says me.
He laughed too.

And off we went our separate ways.

I'm a wee bit happier than before.
But a wee bit sadder too.

24 Jan 2021, 14:21

I filled the car in Top Road garage today, and went and joined the queue to get in. Minding my own business, paying no heed, keeping the head down and my mask up, deciding what to get on my Subway wrap while I was there.

The man behind me spoke. Loudly.
Eighty-eight pound he declared, in astonishment.

I ignored him, I assumed he was talking to someone else.

Eighty-eight pound he declared again, louder and more incredulous.
I still ignored him.

Scuze me he says.
I finally turned around. He was standing right behind me. No 2-metre exclusion zone here. He looked a touch iffy. You know the way you look at some people and immediately know that you just don't like them? I didn't like him.

I'm just saying eighty-eight pound, he enthusiastically declared.
Now ye have it, I says, not really inviting further conversation.
The queue inched forward.

I can't believe you just put eighty-eight pounds of diesel in your car, he declared.
OK says me.
I mean, I put forty-two pound of petrol in my car, and you were there ages longer than me so I went round to check and you had put eighty-eight pound of diesel in your car, he clarified in amazement.
OK says me again.
The queue inched forward.

I can't believe that, I just says that to the wife, that fella just put eighty-eight pound of diesel in his car, I've never seen anyone spend that much on diesel in one go in my life, he declared.
I looked over at the wife, she was indeed staring at me, and appeared to be quite amused.
OK says me.
The queue inched forward.

Eighty-eight pound he declared chuckling away to himself.

I decided I had enough. I turned to face him.

Fort- two pound of petrol I asked?
Yep he declared proudly.
How many miles will you get out of that I asked?
350 he declared proudly, or maybe 400.
350 I repeated incredulously, or maybe even 400????
Yep he declared proudly.

The queue inched forward.

Three fifty miles, I says.
WOW I says.

Is that all, I asked in amazement????

He suddenly wasn't so sure of himself.
He wasn't chuckling anymore.
We inched forward.

I get nine fifty or maybe even a thousand, says me.
I once got a thousand and ninety eight driving easy, says me.
Three=- fifty, I declared chuckling.
WOW, I declared in amazement.
Three-fifty, I chuckled again.
You must be in here a lot, I chuckled.
An AWFUL lot, I declared.
And I gave a big amused satisfied sigh at his teeny tank.

Three-fifty, I chuckled away.

Three-fifty.

Chuckle.

Chuckle.

Funny, I don't think he likes me either. That's why I didn't mention
that nine-fifty would have meant me driving it easy. Very easy. And

filling it again. Ah well.

Three-fifty. I'm still chuckling at them and their teeny tiny tank. Wonder will he tell the wife that???

28 Jan 2021, 20:22

Little things, done right and done regularly, soon become little patterns.

Little patterns, done right and done regularly, soon become little habits.

Little habits, done right and done regularly, soon become lifestyle choices.

Today, for probably the first time in years, I didn't stand at the bottom of a long steep hill thinking I might not make it. Instead, I stood at the bottom of a long steep hill, called it a bitch, hoiked up my big boy pants, and whistled every step of the way, and when I got to the end I thought it was a pity. I was ready, willing and able to do more, and I was midway through a good tune.

I reckon I might be creating a hiking habit.

It started with the little things.

30 Jan 2021, 13:21

Its tough times lads.
You are gonna have days where it just doesn't work. We all will.
You are gonna have days where it just doesn't happen. We all will.

You are gonna have days where it just feels wrong. We all will.
You are gonna have days where it's a long tedious uphill slog. We all will.
You are gonna have days when you struggle. We all will.
You are gonna have days when you are not OK. We all will.

But that's OK.
Do what you need to do to keep going.
It's OK not to feel OK.

Just remember one thing

You will also have days soon where everything is an absolute doddle, where life is great, where the sun is shining, and where everything is a breeze.

We all will.

31 Jan 2021, 12:20

It's the start of February.
It's cold.
It's damp.
It's windy.
We are locked down.
Golf courses are closed.
I'm old.
I'm tired.
I'm cold.
I've got a touch of a toothache.
One of those days.

But then I made breakfast.
Scrambled eggs.

In the same pan as I made curry in over the weekend.
And all I could smell in the kitchen was curry.
But not just any curry.
It was McDonnells curry.
Finest curry known to man.
And the taste.
JAYSUS LADS, THE TASTE!!!
Scrambled eggs and toast flavoured with curry.
With McDonnells curry.
BLISS.

So now.
Stuff the cold, the wind, the damp.
Life is good.
Life is great.
Life is curried.

1 Feb 2021, 10:41

Ahhh working from home.
I find it stompy.

Half 9. I went in to see if the Hells Bells wanted poached eggs and toast. She did. She was free 10.05 to 10.11. I decided to do some work while I was waiting, then make breakfast. I cook, she does dishes. I got distracted She came in at 10.15 looking her breakfast. I said I would stick it on now. But it was too late. She stomped off down the hall to sort herself out. Ah well. My bad

Half 11. She asked what I wanted for lunch. I said I was going to the garage to get stuff for the next few days, and I would get something then. She asked me to get her a plain bloomer and some crisps. OK no probs. Then just after noon she stuck her head round the door and said she didn't realise I was back. I said I hadn't gone yet. She said she was on her lunch and wanted her crisps and plain bloomer. I said I would be on my lunch at 1 and would get it then. She said she would have cuppa soup instead and stomped off down the hall. Ah well. My bad.

1pm. Went to the garage, got shopping, got a bloomer, left the crisps, got myself a wrap, came back. 2pm. She was looking for her crisps. I hadn't gotten her any, because she had cuppa soup instead. I stomped off down the hall. Ah well. Her bad.

5pm I stuck on the dinner. 5.45pm I called her to tell her dinner was ready. I cook, she cleans. She said the plumber is calling. We had been there all day, we were there all evening, and he was calling at the few minutes we were eating. I stomped off down the hall. Ah well. Plumbers bad.

6.15pm. The plumber wanted paid. Fifteen quid. Very cheap. I handed him a twenty and told him to keep the change. He looked at me. Fifty he said. FIFTY he said again. Sorry says me. I thought you said fifteen says me. I chuckled. He didn't. I handed him another thirty quid. He looked at me. I looked at him. He wanted his fiver tip. I didn't offer, I didn't have change. He stomped off down the hall. Ah well. My bad.

9pm. Funny story she says. I actually have crisps in my car she says. I forgot about them till now she says. And she chuckled and chuckled and chuckled.

I just stomped off down the hall.
Ah well.

4 Feb 2021, 10:10

I had to visit the emergency dentist Monday, and it was full of feckin immigrants.

One of them took my Xray, and explained clearly and politely why the tooth needed to go, while another took the tooth out painlessly and swiftly and apologised for keeping me waiting downstairs for all of 3 minutes.

10 Feb 2021, 14:08

We were bickering.
We were jousting.
We were messing.
She made a wild claim that I ignored her or didn't pay her enough attention, or something like that. I don't know, I was only half listening.
So I responded with 'all right Cyrell"

SPOILER You might need to have seen Married at First Sight Australia to get the reference.

She snapped.
But she snapped quietly.
Quiet Nordies are dangerous.
Quiet Nordies are scary.
What did you call me, she asked quietly?
Did you just call me Cyrell, she intoned?
As in the mad, gobby, nut job Cyrell, she dared me?

Now.
I suddenly realised that I had gone too far.
There was a line in the sand, and I had crossed it.
I had crossed it at speed.
I hadn't even seen the line I was crossing.

But I still hadn't stopped.
And I now couldn't see the line in the sand it was so far behind me.
I was in trouble.
And she was daring me to keep going

I tried to save the day.
But without backing down.
I wasn't for backing down.

NOOOOO, says me confidently.
CRYELL, I clarified.
The cute redhead thats always smiling and madly in love with the
Cricket fella and everyone loves them both, says me.
That's Cyrell, says me.
Isn't it, says me innocently?

She thought about it.
She wasn't sure.

That's not Cyrell, she declared.
Are you sure, I asked innocently?
No, that's Jules, she declared.
Ah OK, says me.
Sorry, says me.
All right Jules, I clarified.

I was smug.
I was contented.
I had back pedalled.
I had gotten away with it.
Life was good.

And then she spoke again.

So Jules is a redhead with big hips she declared.
So you were actually calling ME a redhead with big hips, she clarified.

Game over. I lose.
I maybe should have stuck with Cyrell.....

11 Feb 2021, 11:22

I had a big lad with me.
A big lad who struggles with normal life.
A big lad with a big heart and a big personality.

We went out the lane, to turn right.
I asked if there was anything coming from his side.
He was surprised.
He wasn't used to being asked his opinion.
Ignored. Yes.
Side-lined. Yes.
Underestimated. Yes.
But asked his opinion? No.
He sat up, checked the road and told me there was nothing coming.

We came to the end of the road, turning right.
I asked again if there was anything coming from his side.
He seemed surprised again.
He sat up, checked the road and told me there was nothing coming.

I went down the road, planned the route, and realised that there were no more right turns.
So I went round the block, and gained four more right turns.
I asked him in the first right turn if there was anything coming.
And the second right turn.

And the third right turn.
On the fourth right turn he didn't need to be asked.
He told me the road was clear.

It made me smile.

We did a fair few right turns on the way home too. Funny enough.

If people with special needs can't or won't or don't come into our world, we can usually go into theirs. Or we can meet them half way. It will make you smile. You as in plural you. Both of you. Guaranteed.

Take care lads x.

12 Feb 2021, 13:15

The Hells Bells didn't correct me earlier.
It was nice.

But then she told me that she hadn't corrected me.
And then she explained why she hadn't corrected me.
And then she explained why I needed corrected.
And finally she praised herself for not correcting me.

Go her. But I think I preferred the correcting HB......

12 Feb 2021, 14:02

Hey lads.

Adversity makes Achievement even sweeter.

And these are Adverse times.

So just imagine how sweet the Achievements are going to be.
How nice that first meal out is going to taste?
How tight that first hug is going to get?
How good it's going to feel to have a manly handshake with the lads, followed by a squeezy hug, followed by a shy embarrassed smile?
How fine that bottle of red wine pop is going to sound, how sparkly it's going to look, and how sweet it's going to taste?
How long and lively and interesting the chat and banter is going to be?
How foamy that pint is going to look, and how golden is going to taste, from new pipes, in new glasses, from a fresh keg.
How amazing is the buzz in the coffee shops and restaurants and the first tee and the terraces and the pitches and the courts going to be?

Morning all.
Isn't life grand?
Maybe not right now, but its most definitely going to be.

15 Feb 2021, 10:02

Talking to the local Covid deniers/mask avoiders earlier.
It turns out I have it all wrong.

It's all a myth started by the capitalist bankers in league with the communist judges and the deceitful doctors and dishonest nurses and lying medical staff in league with yer man from Microsoft and they are all slowly poisoning us via vaccine and recording us via injected computer chips through the 5g network because the earth is over populated and they want rid of the more knowledgeable people like them so they bombard them with fake trolls, and they know all this because it's on a website called DuckDuckGo.

Sounded fair enough until DuckDuckGo.
I laughed.

They weren't expecting that response.
They thought they had a convert.
They thought I would be on their side.
A fellow visionary.
Their surprise made it funnier.
It tickled my funny bone.
And once I start, I can't stop.
So I laughed harder.
And harder.
And harder.
And even harder.
Duck Duck feckin go!!!!
Everybody is lying to us except Duck Duck feckin go!!!!

I got myself under control.
I apologised for laughing.
Everyone should get a fair hearing.
No matter how stupid they are.

Could you not have thought of a better name I asked?
Like conspiracy uncovered dot com I asked?
Or truth revealed dot co dot UK I asked?
But I mean Duck Duck feckin go???

And off I went again.
Jaysus lads I can't cope with you lot I gasped.

Ah well.

I lost it again when they started talking about freedom (I said
FREEDOM in a bad Scottish accent) and how their four fathers
sailed across the sea and I had to point out that they had one
father, I met him years ago, and he worked in a fruit shop in Belfast
(he had a grand line, what colour apples do ye want, green yellow
or blue, all the kids would giggle and say blue and he would give
them a yellow apple covered in blue paper), he ended up in

Carrickfergus, he never sailed anywhere, and if he did he really should have just taken the M5 instead.
I had to beg them to stop.
I was just too sore.
I had enough for one day.
Duck Duck feckin go!!!!
Classic!!!!

We had the in-laws and their dog Maxie here, they have workmen in the house and for safety and isolation they have had to come to ours for a day.

For themselves (and us) they brought the following:
pancakes for a snack, lovely, it was pancake Tuesday after all.

For the dog they brought the following:
short walking lead,
long walking lead,
in car lead,
harness,
collar,
enough food to do a week,
snacks,
shovel thing for food,
more snacks,
day blanket,
night blanket,
day toy,
night toy,
spare toy,
travel cage to sleep in,
cage toys,
blanket for cage,
bedding for cage,

several bowls,
hairbrush,
beauty products,
sanitary products,
and some more snacks,
finally a few other bits and pieces just in case.

Love it.

17 Feb 2021, 09:03

I took a big lad out with me the other morning.
He hadn't shaved, he hadn't had a haircut, he hadn't dressed up,
and he was still the tidiest looking of the pair of us.

We decided to treat ourselves to a sausage bap from a chippy van
mid-morning.

Few lorry drivers standing round, we joined the queue, the lady
called out, I ordered, I asked him what he wanted, he ordered.
His speech isn't great, but the lady understood.
She understood most of it.
She understood enough of it.
Nice touch.

A lorry driver started chatting to him.
He had heard me say his name, so he used it too.
Nice touch.

Socially distanced chat.
He ignored me, and started chatting directly to him.
Nice touch.

Where were we going today?
What were we doing today?
Isn't it nice to be out and about?

He asked about his family.
Did his mammy know he was getting sausage baps?
He said no and laughed.
Oh boy he would be in trouble when he got home.
He laughed harder.
Nice touch.

Now, when this lad laughs, it's impossible not to join in. His laugh is a big honest wholesome chuckle that starts in his belly and takes over his whole body as it comes out. You just can't not laugh with him. It's just not possible. It just doesn't happen. If he laughs, you laugh. You may not have heard the joke, you may have no idea why you are laughing, but you just find yourself laughing.

They all laughed with him.
So did I.
They told him to blame me for the sausage baps.
He found this hilarious.
And they all laughed along with him.
And so did I, even though I was the one getting grounded by his mammy.
Nice touch.

The lady asked what we wanted on the sausage baps. She asked him directly, and she listened to him carefully, and she waited a second or two for him to answer. She gave him room.
Nice touch.

We got the sausage baps, we ate them in the car, he carried the baps and the drinks back, the lady handed them to him slowly and carefully, the lorry drivers offered to help but didn't insist.
Nice touch after nice touch after nice touch.

We finished and we left, we waved and they all waved back and we beeped and we all smiled.
Nice touch.

When I say they waved, it wasn't just a distracted wave, or an acknowledging finger. It was a genuine big smiley wave, the lady made sure she leaned out of the van so we could see her waving, the drivers all shuffled to one side or the other so we could see them waving too.
Nice touch.

Evening all.
Isn't life grand??
18 Feb 2021, 17:34

Ballyboley Forest.

I take my time going uphill, I don't want to burn myself out. But don't worry, I always get there.

I take my time going downhill, I don't want to fall. But don't worry, I always get there.

I took a couple of hours off to go walking, I just needed to go walking. I know I have a lot of work to do, but don't worry, I always get there too.......

22 Feb 2021, 18:06

One for the boys.
Move along ladies.
Nothing to see here.

Right gents.
Big week next week gents.
Our women folk are going to need us.
Monday evening. About 8pm. Maybe 8.30.
We need to be prepared.
We need to be ready.
They have been good to us, and we need to step up.

Their appetites will change. They may stop eating. Or they could eat the hind leg of the lamb of God. Be ready. Rice cakes and mountains of curry chips should cover most eventualities.

No flowers. Flowers will bring back bad memories. Flowers will hurt.

Chocolate will be good. But not something macho like a Yorkie. Girly chocolate only.

Crisps too. But not strong crisps. No Walkers hot chicken wing ridged crisps. Posh crisps. Crisps that come with dips.

Wine will be essential. Budget 6 bottles. Per female. Per night. And gin. With slimline tonic. Because they may have just eaten the hind leg of the lamb of God. See above. And fruit. Not fruit to eat, fruit for the gin.

The mood will be volatile and irritable. OK, OK I know. Don't say it. Definitely don't put it in writing. But they may be even more volatile and irritable than usual. Volatiler. Irritabler.

Muscle pain, sweating, tremors are to be expected. For a few days, maybe a few weeks. Probably from both of you. But it's OK. You will get through this.

Don't say anything contentious.
Don't speak of kangaroos, Australia, weddings, Jessie, Martha,

neighbours (did you know that Erinsborough is an anagram of neighbours??) (I didn't!!)
Feel free to say 'I really hope it works out for Cam and Jules'
Or 'Mike is a prat'
And then let them talk. Talking will help. It's good to talk.

You see, they are all hooked on Married at First Sight Australia season 6 which has been going on and on for months. And it's about to stop. Monday evening. 8pm. Maybe 8.30pm. Be warned. Be ready. The ladies will need us.

Oh and don't tell them that Neighbours thing either. No matter how tempted you are. It won't help.

Season 7 comes in the summer. Roll on summer.

23 Feb 2021, 22:31

I was out for a walk, and I met a funeral procession.
Hearse and four cars coming towards me.
Small funeral.

I stopped.
I faced the cortege.
I bowed my head in respect.
I waited about 5 seconds for the family to pass, and resumed my walk.
I got a wee nod of thanks from the last car.

Family is limited at funerals.
Friends are limited at funerals.
But maybe you will find yourself in a position to show a bit of respect for someone's final journey.
Please take the opportunity.

Please pause and show respect in whatever way you can

I think I would appreciate it if I was one of the mourners, or if the deceased was one of my family or friends.
I think we all would.

Take care.

24 Feb 2021, 11:43

I like people.
Bear with me.
This may appear a bit mean, but it's not intended to, its intended to be a compliment.

I have a wee elderly man that volunteers to do books for a wee church group.
Except he struggles to do books.
So many years ago he asked me to help.
And I did.
But we couldn't let on that he needed help.
And he wanted to pay me for my time.
So I said I could send an invoice to the church group.
And he said no, he wanted to pay me himself.
And I said no, in that case I didn't want paid.
And he got annoyed at me working for nothing.
And I got annoyed at the idea of him having to pay.
So we agreed he would do a wee bit of electrical work instead.
Quid pro quo.
And I would keep doing the books.
Sorted.

He put up a socket, he put up few lights, he fitted a few bulbs for the first few years, and we had the chat, the craic, and the tea.
Sorted.
Then one year he brought an outside light because he felt that we

had a dark corner, and we had the chat, the craic, and the tea.
Sorted.
Then the next year he brought a floodlight for the side of the house.
A big floodlight. A big bright industrial floodlight. And we had the
chat, the craic, and the tea.
Sorted.
Then he brought another outside light, so we put it up over the
back door at the decking, because DHL drivers were going blind out
the front. And ditto the chat etc.
Sorted.
Then another light, it too went over the decking. And ditto the craic
etc.
And so the years went on.
And the lights went on. And the tea went on.

Last year the lights on the decking were so bright, I took the bulb
out of one of them.
This year he saw that, and replaced the bulb, and left me a spare
one just in case.
And then he fitted yet another light.
That doesn't match a single one of the other 5 lights in that wee
corner.
Nor any of the 7 lights on the other side.
Some are white, some are blue, some are LED, some are filament,
some are sensor, some are solar, but they all work.
When I turn them on EasyJet pilots circle overhead thinking the
International Airport has moved, and Kilroot Power Station goes on
overtime.

Anyway, I love them.

I love them, because for me they remind me of a wee man that
wants a bit of help but needs to pay his way. Or maybe he needs a
bit of help, and wants to pay his way. And have the chat, the craic
and the tea.

Afternoon all.
Isn't life grand????

Proper Tayto have released two new flavours.
In proper Tayto land.
But I'm stuck here with the Nordies.
In Cardboard Crisp land.
I'm in lockdown.
There is a 58 mile drive in a 10 mile limit and a Garda checkpoint
with a 100 euro fine between me and the new flavours.
And the Nordies are loving it.
I'm getting teased.
I'm getting laughed at.
Incessantly.

I still reckon a 100 Euro fine could be worth it.

I blame the television.
The Nordies are giddy.
They are getting uppity.
They are always on the tele these days you see.
The had Marcella here. So they did.
Then Bloodlines (even though they complained that it wasn't
Nordie enough, so it wasn't)
Then DIY SOS. So it was.
And there is a Nordie in Corrie. So there is.
And Line of Duty is being shown soon. So it is.
Followed by Derry Girls. Which is all about girls. From Londonderry.
I can't see much respite ahead. So I cant.
The coldest winter I ever spent was last summer in Carrickfergus. So
it was.

Ah well. I have no choice. Grin and bear it. Here is me what. That is
us now. As they say in these parts.

She is quiet.
She isn't talking much.
She seems to be in good enough form.
But she just isn't saying much.
She seems distant.
Reserved.
Detached.
Don't know what happened.

We had a nice day.
We had a nice walk with the dog.
Then we had a glass of wine before dinner.
Then we had a nice dinner with another nice glass of wine.
Then we opened another bottle of wine.
Then we had wine gums.
Then we finished that bottle of wine.

I needed to pee.
She told me it was my round.
I told her the wine bottle was empty.
She smiled at me cheekily.
I asked her what she wanted.
She smiled at me coyly.
I told her I had enough wine, I fancied something different.
She smiled at me saucily.
She told me she would have whatever I was having.
Ok I agreed.

I was having a Coke Zero.
So I brought her one as well.
Since then, silence.
Can't think why..............

So love says me.
Last day in your forty eights says me.
Birthday tomorrow says me.
What would you like to do tonight says me?
Wine and a nice meal says me?
I will cook says me?
And even clean up afterwards says me?
Or a takeaway says me?
Nice romantic evening says me?
We can't go out, no one can come here says me.
Gas fire, dim the lights, bit of Marty Mone, glass of wine, snuggle on the sofa, says me?

She thought about it.

She thought some more.

Then she spoke.

There is one thing I would like she says.

Woohoo I thought.
Here we go I thought.
Brace yourself big man I thought.
But I didn't let it show.
I didn't rub my hands together or lick my lips or anything obvious like that.
I played it cool.
Yes love says me?
Anything you want says me.

Well she says?
Any chance.....she says?

You could.....she says?

Yes love says me?

Make yourself scarce, she says.
I have plans, she says.

Ah well.
Might as well go for a walk.
Burn off some frustrated energy.

2 Mar 2021, 18:56

So Pontins have banned certain Irish surnames from booking.
Banned people include:

Sean Boylan, who won 4 All Ireland as coach with Meath, one of the true greats in GAA.

Danny Boyle, director of Trainspotting and Slumdog Millionaire among others, Olympic opening ceremony, and Knighthood offeree and decliner. Respect.

Peader Kearney, author of the Irish National Anthem. Can't sing in Pontins. Rob Kearney and Brian Carney, Rugby legends. Can't play in Pontins.

Alan Carr. English comedian. See how ridiculous this is getting? Jimmy Carr. Irish English comedian. Quare laugh. Tax legend. Probably correct. Norman Carr MBE. Conservationist. MB feckin E, but can't get into Pontins.

Pat Cash. Won Wimbledon. Can't get into Pontins. Neither can Johnny Cash, the Man in Black.

Jimmy Connor. What is it about Wimbledon winners?

William Corcoran. Washington DC Philanthropist. Art gallery. Donated heating to the poor. All round decent spud.

Thomas Delaney, Borussia Dortmund Danish footballer. He will be gutted. Also a man that's called Delany, owner of a chipped yellow JCB. He could help build Pontins, but can't visit Pontins.

Gemma Doherty. How could anyone not like, if not love, Gemma Doherty??

Liam and Noel Gallagher. Sorry lads. Pat the Cope Gallagher. How will he cope?

Niall Horan. Singer, songwriter, second best in Mullingar. Fair enough, he's no Joe Dolan.

Jonathan Rhys Meyers. Born O Keefe, good enough for Hugo Boss, but not for Pontins.

Vernon Kell. He founded MI5, but Pontins have his measure.

Sir John Leahy and Sir Terry Leahy. Welcome at the Palace, not at Pontins.

Bruce Lee, Stan Lee, Robert E Lee, Spike Lee, Harper Lee, Lee Jeans, the General Lee, Lee Martin, Lee Westwood, Lee Harvey Oswald. All outstanding in their fields. High achievers. Successful. Until now.

A McLaughlin designed the flag of the United Nations. A McLaughlin became one of the greatest ever managers in the League of Ireland. A McCully went to space. The author Donagh McDonagh is doubly devastated. Paul McGinley won the Ryder Cup, but can't play crazy golf in Pontins. Not anymore.

Jim McGuinness. You excluded Jim from Pontins. And you spelled his name wrong. Jaysus, it's just insult after insult with you lot, isn't it?

Vince McMahon. As in the WWE wrestling McMahon family. You specialise in fake, cheap, tatty, enjoyable entertainment, but exclude possibly the fakest, cheapest, tastiest, most enjoyable entertainer of all?

Spike Milligan. Goonie. You are looking at the Goonies and judging them not suitable? You? Pontins judging the Goonies? Jaysus.

Eddie Murphy, Cillian Murphy, Irish Stout Murphy, Spud Murphy, Granny Murphy, Robocop, all excluded from your grubby little club.

The Nolan sisters, and them in their tight black trousers. Really? Really?

O Brien, O Connell, O Donnell, O Donoghue, O Mahony, O Reilly. Some great rugby names there. They could fill a dance floor on their own. And Obama of course. Irish. Starts with an O. Bound to be banned.

Sheridan and Stokes. There are 25 places called after Sheridans in the States, but not a Sheridan in Pontins. Hmmm.

Bradley Walsh. And Girls Aloud. And Shane Ward. And Geriatric Ward. Paediatric Ward. Even Oncology Ward. Not welcome. Can't book. Really?

Really? And this was your official policy? For six years?

Meanwhile your founder Fred Pontin, left school with no qualifications or examinations, dragged himself up and up and up and donated millions to charity. He became a Sir. You took over his company. But these days you probably would ban him too as undesirable.

Really?

Wee daughter phoned me.

Daddy she says?
I'm doing the 4 peaks in March she says.
I'm going to do Divis tonight she says.
Do you fancy coming she says?

No says me.
Definitely not says me.
I did a big hike yesterday says me.
And my feet are sore says me.
Cos I wore the wrong shoes says me.
And the stones nipped me through the shoes says me.
And my legs are tired says me.
We did a bit of climbing yesterday says me.
And it's very dark says me.
And cold says me.
Especially on top of a mountain says me.
Brrrrr says me.
And there will be showers says me.
There is rain forecast says me.
And I have loads of work says me.
I haven't had my dinner says me.
And I want to watch the football says me.
So count me out says me.
Definitely not says me.
No says me.

And that's how I ended up on top of Divis with the wee daughter.

4 Mar 2021, 20:50

Wee daughter phoned the Hells Bells

Mummy she says?
I'm doing the 4 peaks in March she says.
I'm going to do Cavehill today she says.
Do you fancy coming she says?

I smirked to myself.

No says HB.
Definitely not says HB.
It's cold says HB.
Especially on top of a mountain says HB.
Brrrrr says HB.
I chuckled to myself.
And I have loads of work says HB.
I haven't had my dinner says HB.
And I need to do housework says HB.
I laughed to myself.
So count me out says HB.
Definitely not says HB.
No says HB.

I laughed and laughed and laughed.

And then somehow I ended up on top of Cavehill with the Hells

Bells and the wee daughter.
I wasn't laughing anymore.

7 Mar 2021, 16:13

Meghan Markle, Prince Harry, Piers Morgan.

In my experience, people don't lie about being anxious, anxious people lie about being OK.
In my experience, people don't lie about being depressed, depressed people lie about being OK.
In my experience people don't lie about being suicidal, suicidal people lie about being OK.

If someone says they are anxious, or depressed, or suicidal, they aren't telling lies. They are crying out for understanding and help. In my experience.

8 Mar 2021, 21:01

I owe the Nordies a wee apology.
I may have been a wee bit dismissive about Nordie Tayto.
And I want to apologise.

I have learned that it's all about context.
I was comparing Nordie Tayto unfavourably against Proper Tayto.
That wasn't fair. There is no comparison.

However when I recently combined a bag of cross community Nordie Tayto with a couple of bottles of alcohol free lager (driving) I had a perfectly pleasant plain, bland, boring, tasteless, average afternoon snack. Apart from the beer. The beer was actually really, really good.

Afternoon all.

There's a place for everything, and everything has a place, even Nordie Tayto, meat free burgers, tofu, decaf tea, alcohol free beer and such like. I see that now.
So I apologise.
Isn't life grand?
Bland, but grand?

13 Mar 2021, 21:41

Wee daughter phoned me. Wee daughter is climbing 4 mountains in March.

Daddy she says?

I recognised the tone. I didn't let her speak.

No says me.
I'm not doing it says me.
I don't care what it is says me.
I don't care where it is says me.
I'm not doing it says me.
You are not going to talk me round this time says me.
No point trying says me.
The big eyes are not going to work says me.
I'm old says me.
I'm unfit says me.
I'm tired says me.
The answer is no says me.
You have a boyfriend says me.
Take him says me.
Make him says me.
It's his job now says me.
My work here is done says me.
I am definitely not climbing any mountains says me.
Final answer says me.
Don't ask again says me.

I'm putting my foot down on this one says me.

And that's how I somehow ended up on top of Slieve Doan in the Mournes.
With the wee daughter.
And the boyfriend.

15 Mar 2021, 17:02

I turned down the road towards the funeral home.
A funeral director stepped out.
I had to stop.
I groaned inwardly.
I had to wait.
It would have been bad manners to pass.
A hearse moved slowly out.
I waited for the rest of the cortege.

But there wasn't one.

There was an undertaker walking.
There was a hearse with a coffin.
That was all.
No limousine, no mourners, no cars, no procession.

The undertaker walked slowly down the road along the route they always take.
The hearse followed.
I followed at a respectful distance.
The undertaker stopped 100 yards from the funeral home where they always stop.
The hearse stopped.
I stopped at a respectful distance.
The undertaker walked round the back of the hearse, checked the back door, and got into the passenger seat, and they left.
I left after a respectful pause.

And I thought it was a very simple, touching, caring, professional, dignified and respectful send off.
Especially as there was no cortege, no mourners, no witnesses.
Except them.
And me.

Well done to all.

17 Mar 2021, 20:35

Do you want a cuppa says me?
Aye she says.
And a bickie says me?
Nah she says.
You sure says me?
Aye she says.
Just a cuppa says me?
Aye she says.

I went to make the tea.
I buttered 2 digestives for myself.
I thought about it.
I reckoned she would want some.
I buttered two more.

I brought her in tea.
No bickies.
I brought in my tea.
And 4 bickies.

And she supped and I supped and nibbled.
She looked at the bickies.
I avoided eye contact.
She looked away.
We supped on.

She looked again.
I ignored her.
She looked away.
We supped on.

She looked again.
I caught her eye.
You want one says me?
She thought about it.
Aye she says.
I gave her a bickie.
Sharing's caring she says, gloating.
Hmmm says me, huffily.

She is happy.
She has tea
She has bickies.
She got one over on me.

I too am happy.
I too have tea.
I too have bickies.
And I was proved right.

Evening all.
It's a wild life we lead, but we wouldn't have it any other way.

18 Mar 2021, 20:25

I love this wee place.

I went to the garage for breakfast.
Lady in front of me in the queue.
She ordered 2 sausage baguettes, one with crispy bacon, one with
veggie roll, one with two sausages, one with three, one with a soft

egg, one with a hard egg, one with ketchup, one with brown, all very complicated.
And she ordered it as a grunt.
She ordered it as if she was being put out by having to order.
She ordered it as if she was being put out by having to open her mouth to speak.

I ordered too from the second server. The second server is my mate. I visit her weekly. We are deli buddies. She has eyes that glint with mischief. She knows what I like, and I say please and thank you and take what I am given. Two sausage sandwiches on brown bread with ketchup please. Nice and easy.
And we waited.

The servers made hers and mine.
She got her sausage baguettes, she got her crispy bacon and veggie roll, she got her soft egg on one, she got her hard egg on the other, and then it all went wrong. Her server apparently put brown sauce on the wrong baguette.

The customer sprang into life.
Her diction became clearer.
She became animated.
She became angry.
Well!!! she demanded.
That's just the wrong sauce!!! she declared.
You will have to make that again from scratch!!! she decided.
This however seemed to please her. She had found someone beneath her. She had found someone at her behest. Someone she could boss around. Someone she could give out to. Someone she could treat like crap. And she seemed to like that.

Her server started to remake her baguette.

Anyway my sausage sandwiches were ready.
With big smiles and thanks.

From them and from me.
Aren't we just the loveliest people ever?
The other customer just stood moody, ignored, scowling, waiting.

Then my deli buddy played a master stroke.

Sir, she says?
Yes, says me?
Do you want this one too, she asked indicating the one with the brown sauce.
On the house, she asked?
You can have it or else we have to put it in the bin, she declared.
This lady doesn't want it, she declared.

I looked at the customer.
Her face was a picture.
This wasn't part of her plan
Awww tanks says me.
I will take it surely says me.
And I took it.
And I smiled in appreciation to the other customer.
She just scowled at me.
That made it even sweeter.

See you next week, deli buddy.

I just love this wee mad stupid bonkers place and it's crazy people.
Often derided, but seldom defeated.

19 Mar 2021, 11:53

Complete moonbeam on the phone this morning.

He wants the self-employed grant, but he never registered as self-employed, and he never submitted tax returns, and never paid a penny in tax and NIC.

I asked him why he never registered.

He explained to me in great detail that under the terms of the Magna Carta the King only has the right to tax by consent of the people, and he had refused to give his consent. He was surprised that a man in my trade didn't know all about this approach.

I didn't bother arguing, I ceded to his superior knowledge. He appeared to be one of those.

Now ye have it says me.

No point arguing with stupid, he is hugely experienced, and I am only barely qualified.

Anyway he needed me to fix it all. He also needed me to bill HMRC for the work, after all they were the ones asking for it.

I declined. Too much work on my side, not enough time, too much expertise on his side, not enough knowledge.

He seemed upset.

He seemed angry.

He seemed to believe that he had the right to refuse consent, but I didn't have that exact same right.

I didn't bother arguing. I ceded to his superior knowledge.

Now ye have it says me.

Anyway, after several minutes of him moaning and complaining and demanding and haranguing and me saying now ye have it, now ye have it, now ye have it, I changed tack.

I expressed my deep respect and admiration for him, and that he is costing himself so much money every year to stand up for his principles.

He seemed surprised.

Men like him are few and far between.

He seemed agreeable to this.

He had cost himself sick pay, state pension, and tax credits worth £6k a year (family, 2 children, low income) and all to save submitting a tax return and paying £400 national insurance payment a year.

He seemed confused. He seemed surprised. He didn't seem to realise this.
Then I told him that I could never help a man betray his principles.
He tried to interrupt.
Then I told him to stick to his guns.
He tried to speak.
Then I hung up.
Then I blocked his number.

Magna Carta!!
Now ye have it.
24 Mar 2021, 10:51

I love the simple things in life.
The little things.
The small things.
Order.
Organisation.
Symmetry.
Control.

Take this morning for example.

Breakfast time.
I used the last of the milk.
I used the last of the cheese.
I used the last of the ham.
This pleased me immensely.
Perfect symmetry.
Perfect control.
Perfection.

So then I put all the empty wrappers back in the fridge just to drive the Hells Bells batshit crazy.
For a bit of chaos.

For a bit of passion.
For a bit of whimsy.
That pleases me immensely too.

Simple things.

It's been a good symmetrical morning, it's gonna be a giddy
whimsical evening.

Line of Duty.

Why did they have to call him Ted?
Of all the names they could have, they had to pick Ted.
They had many choices.
Hundreds and hundreds of names.
Tom.
We wouldn't have objected to Tom
Or Tim.
Tim is a nice name.
But no.
They had to have Ted.
Ted is our name.
Our wee Father Ted.
Are ye right there Ted?
Looks like rain Ted.
Ahhh that's mad Ted.
The most perfect Ted ever.

Now the Nordies have their own Ted.
Ted Hastings.
Ted the Tout.

And every time I say 'Are ye right there Ted?' she answers in a
Nordie way.

Here's me wha, she says.
Suckin diesel, she says.
Or worst of all.
I didn't come up the Lagan in a bubble, she says.

But I'm not doing your Ted.
I'm doing my Ted.
I don't want an answer from your Ted.
I want an answer from my Ted.

So again, why did it have to be Ted?

Ted.
Ruined for ever.
Are ye right there Ted?
Houl yer whist.

27 Mar 2021, 22:22

I had been up the Mournes, and the face was beet red. I had pulled on a pair of shorts for the first time this year, they were a touch tight, with my scrawny pale legs looked iffy poking out underneath. I had pulled in a t-shirt that had been washed and dried many times, it had faded and stretched and shrunk, and was perilously close to what the young'uns would call a crop top. I was OK as long as I walked with a stoop, that way T-shirt and the shorts met in the middle. Standing up straight was risky. And I couldn't bend down, the shorts were too clingy for bending. But we were in the house for the evening, we had no plans, we weren't going out, nobody was coming in, and I was banjaxed.

And then big son suggested a walk.

Now.
I go walking most days.
Woodburn Forest.

Cavehill.
Carrick Harbour.
Whitehead.
Anywhere local.
And I never meet anyone I know.
Never.
I get the odd beep, and the odd wave, and the odd nod, but never stop to have a chat.
Never.
People I know by and large don't go walking.
The people that walk by and large don't know me.

So I figured I wouldn't bother changing.
My clothes were upstairs, and stairs were not my friend after the days exertions.
And I never meet anyone.
Jacket on, stoop on, and let's go.
We would be grand, right?

Wrong.

Neighbours, ex neighbours, clients, ex clients, school mammys, school daddy's, school teachers, computer guys, friends, acquaintances, enemies, mortal enemies, all out walking on the nice evening, all stopping to say hello, dozens and dozens of them. And me with my pale scrawny legs, my beet red face, my pounced stoop, my inability to bend, and my shuffling, tired, crampy gait.

But do you know something?

It was like pre Covid.
It was like old times.
It was lovely to chat to people.
It was a wee touch of normality.
It was feckin brilliant.

31 Mar 2021, 08:17

I was in a shop with a client.
A client who is also a mate.
A big lad walked in, skin head, battered scarred face, scruffy tracksuit, shuffling gait.
He started talking.
He started telling stories.
He started telling stories about school.
15 years before.
I was surprised they were in school together.
They didn't look remotely the same age.
He told of how he used to pick on my client.
My client just smiled.
He said that my client was a weedy wee fella.
My client just smiled.
He told of how they once stole his trousers and threw them up on the school roof.
My client just smiled.
He told of how they laughed as my client had to climb onto the roof in his pants and retrieve the trousers.
My client just smiled.
He told of how they roared laughing as the trousers were caught on barbed wire and ripped and he had to come back down with trousers with one torn leg and wear them for the rest of the day.
My client just smiled.
He told me of the nickname they had for my client, it wasn't very flattering.
My client just smiled.
On and on and on he went. Belittling. Slobbering. Ridiculing. Denigrating.
My client just smiled. And smiled. And smiled.

When he eventually left, I asked my client why he took that crap.
Especially in his own shop.
In front of his staff.
Why didn't he tell the fella where to go?

Why did he put up with that shite?
What was he scared of?

My client just smiled.

I have a nice business, nice house, nice family, nice car, nice life, he
said.
He doesn't have anything like that he said.
He doesn't have anything else, he said.
All he has is that shite, he said.
From years ago, he said.
Might as well let him have it, he said.

And he just smiled.
Happy, safe and confident.

3 Apr 2021, 01:32

I was spraying the fence.
The Hells Bells came out.
She watched me for a minute.

You know she says......
Aye says me????
I was reading up about this she says......
And says me????
They said that if you spray side to side you use less paint she says.
What do you mean says me????
Show me says me????

So she did.

Look, she says.
This way, she says.
Left and right, she says.

I think I see what you mean, says me.
Show me another bit, says me.

And I went to get a can of Coke Zero.

Oh I see what you mean now, says me sitting sipping my ice cold Coke Zero.

I'm getting the hang of it now, says me finishing off the Coke Zero.

Left and right then right and left, says me edging inside.

Great job, I called from inside the door.

Playing a blinder love, as I turned on the tele. Top Gear. Nepal special.

That's lovely pet, says me putting out the recliner.

Lovely jubbly, says me contemplating a wee nap.

Left and right pet, then right then left, I see what you mean, grand job, lovely jubly, heres me wha, says me sleepily.

(I didn't come up the Lagan in a feckin bubble either pet)

Nite all. Don't forget to say how nice the fence is if you are passing. She has worked hard.

4 Apr 2021, 12:50

I went out to wash my car.
I sprayed it down, then started with the soapy cloth.
Wee daughter saw me.
Wee daughter made a hint about getting her car washed.
Wee daughter gave me the big eyes.

I pretended not to notice.
But the big eyes are powerful things.
Even when you can't see them, you know they are there.
So I decided I might give the wee daughters car a quick splash and dash first.
Or maybe it was decided for me.
Whatever.
Anyway it's only a tiny wee car.
So, I sprayed her car down.
I scrubbed it with the soapy cloth to remove any marks.
And I rinsed it off.
It was lovely.

Wee daughter came out.
Wee daughter pretended to be surprised, but she wasn't really.
She pretended not to be pleased, but she actually was.
And off she went.
Her and the big eyes.

I started again on my car.
I sprayed it down, then started with the soapy cloth.
The Hells Bells saw me.
The Hells Bells made a hint about getting her car washed.
The Hells Bells gave me the big eyes.
I pretended not to notice.
No chance HB.
Don't even bother HB.
Those big eyes don't work on me HB.
You need to get the wee daughter to ask instead......

6 Apr 2021, 19:52

I'm in no rush.
I'm not trying to beat any other walkers.
I'm not trying to beat any other hikers.

I'm not trying to beat any other runners.
I'm not trying to beat any other cyclists.

I'm just trying to climb this mountain.
I'm only trying to beat the sniping little voice that tells me that I can't do this.
That I can't climb a mountain top to bottom.
That I'm too old.
That I'm too unfit.
That it's too steep.
That I'm far too busy.
That I've too much work on.
That it's going to rain.
That it's very cold.
That it's very windy.

Anyway I usually rest when I need to, but today I didn't need to.
I usually stop to look at the view when I want to, but today I didn't want to.
Also I've just realised something.
I lost something.
I misplaced something.
Somewhere between the bottom of the mountain and the top of mountain I mislaid that sniping little voice.
I can't seem to hear it anymore.

Good.

Afternoon all. Its baltic, blowy and brilliant up here.

7 Apr 2021, 16:26

Nice wee things that spring into your mind for no obvious or apparent reason.

Daddy?

Yes pet.
Any chance of a lift to Abbey Centre?
Yes pet.
Now?
Yes pet.
Meet you outside in 5 minutes?
Yes pet.
Love you Daddy.
Yes pet.

I thought about it.

Emma?
Yes Daddy.
See if I'm not outside in 10 minutes?
Yes Daddy.
You go on without me, and I will meet you there.
Yes Daddy.

Then she thought about it.

You're soooo not funny Daddy.
I know pet.
Love you Daddy.
Love you too pet.
□□□□

11 Apr 2021, 13:51

Ah Jaysus lads, this made me smile. Love it. Absolutely love it.

I was working near me Mammys, so I popped my head in the door for a socially distanced visit, and she gave me a bite of lunch and a bit of fruit loaf. She said the fruit loaf was a wee bit dry, it had been left in the oven too long. She had stuck it in the oven, they went to Mass, the Mass lasted longer than they thought, and when she

went to take it out it was a wee bit overdone and a wee bit dry. She knew it was going to be, she knew the Priest was in no rush.
Technically it was all the Priest's fault.
Personally I thought it was very tasty.

I asked what Mass they were at, because you need Presale tickets with allocated seating to go to Mass these days. I believe there's a mighty rush when the tickets are released.
But they weren't physically at Mass, the Mass was on the computer.
The Mass was on YouTube.
I thought this was lovely too.

I made the point that she could have nipped out at Communion and taken the cake out of the oven and nipped back for the final prayers.
She wasn't impressed.
She wasn't the sort of person that would be seen leaving Mass early, with the Priest blessing her backside as she went out the door.
Even if the Mass was on YouTube.
And she wasn't that happy with me for even thinking things like that.
I thought this was the loveliest of all.

Afternoon lads, the sun is shining, and the standards are being kept high. The Mammys have it sorted.

15 Apr 2021, 16:12

A lad told me last week that I was lucky, that my life is so simple, and that's why I'm able to get great joy and enthusiasm from the simple little things like walking and cycling.

I agreed with him that I am indeed lucky.
Even though he said it with a sneer.

So I told him that he was unlucky, his life is so filled with trinkets, but he is perpetually and permanently bored.

And I said that with a smile.

Ah well.
Sunshine.
Forests.
Lakes.
Hills.
Walking.
Isn't a wee bit of simplicity grand?

21 Apr 2021, 16:35

I was chilling on the recliner, I was half asleep, I was splayed out, I was nice and relaxed and at peace with the world.

The Hells Bells was pottering.

She walked past me and dropped the TV remote into my lap on the way past, in case I wanted to change the channel.
I say lap, but you could say crotch.
Ouch I went.
She giggled.
Good shot I went, sarcastically.
Small target she replied, not sarcastically.

I settled back down.

She walked past me from the other direction, and dropped my mobile into my lap on the way past, in case I needed it.
I say lap, but again you could say crotch.
Ouch I went again.
She giggled again.
Two out of two she said.

I settled back down.

She walked back past me again, coming back her original direction, and dropped the house phone into my lap on the way past, in case it rang.
I say lap, but you could say crotch.
OUCH I went.
She giggled harder.
AND ITS THREE FOR THREE she declared.

I settled back down again.

Until out of the settled, sleepy, hazy, dozey corner of my eye I saw her coming towards me carrying the iron.

I decided it might be time to get up.......

24 Apr 2021, 12:12

Anyway.

I got a lift from the Hells Bells to Whitehead, we both did the lighthouse walk, and I decided to walk home alone.
I was wandering up the hill towards Carrickfergus when a couple of walkers came behind me.
They started to chat.

General stuff.
Where you going?
Carrick?
Us too.
Train station and get the train back for them.
I got a lift down and I'm walking back to the car now.

But here's the thing.

They wanted to tell me all about them, but didn't want to hear anything about me.
They were those sort of people.
They looked at me like I was dirt.
But that's Ok.
Their loss.
They didn't like me.
I didn't like them.
I'm big and scruffy and messy and in office socks and un-ironed t shirt and 4 for 20 quid big boy sweatpants.
Their disdain was obvious.
They were dismissive.
He was a muscle man in branded matching gym gear, with water bottles and backpack.
She had spent ages on her makeup, and then walked out without her smile.
Or much personality.
I suspect I kept my disdain better hidden, but truth be told, I didn't try too hard.

So I slowed down, and let them wander ahead.

He seemed pleased at this. They both did.
I didn't blame him.
He seemed competitive. They both did.
I'm not.
He seemed like he had to win. They both did.
I don't.

But here's the thing.
Big muscles and long walks and steep hills don't go together.
I'm getting used to my 10 mile hikes with a few hills, despite appearances.
They are used to short sharp power bursts.
Gym muscles.

Anyway we turned uphill past the garage, them in front, me 20 yards behind, them pumping, me loping, him checking back on me, me whistling and ignoring.
Look forward, not back lads.
We reached the Bla Hole still on much the same positions, me still whistling but only out of bravado now, and them really starting to feel it.

I increased my pace, they started to slow, I caught them up, so they stopped to get a drink at the lay-by. Better to be passed in the pits than on the track. I stopped too, took a quick photo, and moved on again.
They had a quick confab, and started again about 20 yards behind me.
There seemed to be dissent in the camp.
She wanted to turn back.
He didn't
They weren't happy.
I grinned to myself.

We reached the top of the hill, downhill all the way now, I increased my pace and lengthened stride. I was rolling along rightly.
They weren't.
I could hear the slap slap of their feet on the footpath.
It sounded painful.
I was rolling and strolling and cruising it out and grinning.
They were pumping it out, and grimacing.

We passed Jack Reid cars, them still about 20 yards behind me, and them still working hard.
We came to the spot where the footpath ends, and we had to cross the road.
I had to wait.
I pretended to be surprised to see them there.
I spoke to them, cheerily.
They didn't answer.

They glared at me.
They were in pain.
Matching gear was soaked in sweat.
Sore feet.
The backpack was now getting heavy.
I knew the signs.
I've been there.
Many times.

The road cleared and off we went again.

I upped the pace again.
I was now powerwalking.
They started to drop back very slightly.
Their race was run.
They were losing.
To a big whistling eejit in big boy pants and office socks.
And they didn't like it in the slightest.

I crossed the narrow bridge at the salt works, and started really
pushing it on.
I had to check both ways.
They were now 50 yards behind and bickering.
I came into Kilroot at a jog.

Now.
To their credit, they almost stuck with me.
They shouldn't have, but they did.
I sped past Kilroot heading for the corner of the Beltoy.
And there I stopped.
Partly because I was bolloxed.
But mostly because that is where I had left my car that morning.
Technically when I said I was walking to Carrickfergus, I hadn't lied.
I had walked to Carrickfergus.
Outer limits.
The very outer limits.

And they still had 2.6 miles to go to the train station.
I checked this on the map.
I thought about telling them, but decided not to.

I waited for them to pass.
I happily wished them good day.
They didn't reply.
I cheerily wished them Buen Camino.
They didn't reply.
I gave them a beep beep as I drove past.
They didn't wave.

Ah well.
Next time I go to the gym they can get their revenge.
26 Apr 2021, 09:56

Stopped in to Dungannon to get a couple of Ninety Nines, and
ended up meeting the loveliest wee Tyrone girl.

2 Ninety Nines please, says me confidently.
Sorry, she says.
No Ninety Nines, she says.

I looked at the other till where a customer was just leaving with 2
Ninety Nines. I don't like to be a difficult customer, but the issue
had to be raised.

That lady has Ninety Nines, says me, deflated.
No she says.
That lady has two ordinary cones, she says.
She wanted Ninety Nines but I told her we had no Ninety Nines, so
she took ordinary cones instead, she says.

I searched her face for sarcasm, but was happy to find none.

So you are OK with ordinary cones says me.
Yes she says.
But no Ninety Nines says me.
No she says.
Why says me?
No wee flakes left she says.
Ahhh, says me.

I searched her face for signs of a piss take, but was happy to find none.

In that case, can I have two ordinary cones please says me.
This made her happy.
Certainly she says.
Would you like sauce she says?

For a second I thought she meant Ketchup or Brown.
I thought about making a joke of it.
But I decided not to.
She might actually do it.
Strawberry on one please, says me.
She made the cones.
She put Strawberry sauce all over one of them.
She brought them back over.

Now, she says, nodding and holding up the cone that was covered in strawberry sauce.
That's the one with the sauce, she says helpfully.

I searched her face for signs of rudeness or belligerence, but found nothing but sweetness and innocence.

Thanks says me, and took the cones.

And, as an afterthought, while I was leaving, I turned and called

back to her.
These look absolutely lovely, says me.
Thanks a million, says me.

And the wee Tyrone girl was delighted. But so was I. I liked her.

3 May 2021, 21:04

I was going to do Darkness into Light last night, but I was genuinely worried about meeting the wee daughter staggering home with a kebab......

8 May 2021, 22:09

Here's the thing.
People with depression usually don't like themselves very much.

Here's another thing
People with depression always are surprised that you DO like them.

Here's the last thing.
If you want to help someone that is depressed, just show them that you like them. Whatever way you can. Show you care.

Sorted.

11 May 2021, 17:37

Anyway.

I was heading to the city centre, I came in the M2, over the M4 and swung down past the Odyssey and in that way.
Wee blue Fiesta in front of me on the M3 off slip.
Then an Audi estate.

Then me.
Bit slow but grand.

Now.
When you see a wee blue Fiesta with plastic wheel trims, you know usually it's a learner or an older person.
Am I right?
It's usually a nervous driver?
Am I right?
You give them a bit of room?
Am I right?
It's obvious?
Isn't it?

Anyway the Fiesta moved into the left lane.
The lane for the entrance to the Odysssey car park.
And then realised quite late that the lane was closed.
So the Fiesta started to drift back right even though indicating left.
You with me?
Grand.
No?
That's grand too.

The Audi in front saw this happening.
And the Audi planted the accelerator.
I saw the arse drop and a plume of black smoke.
Then the Audi slammed on the brakes.
I saw the arse rise and the brake lights snap on.
And he blared the horn.
And he gesticulated.
Repeatedly.
Aggressively.
Needlessly.
And shouted and yelled and ranted and raved from behind the Fiesta.
For very little reason.

But he had to accelerate hard to put himself in a position where he was able to be put out and slam on the brakes.
What a dick.

But anyway.
Not my circus, not my monkeys.

We moved on, the wee Fiesta stayed in the slow lane and turned into the Covid carpark at the Odyssey, the Audi estate headed for the city centre, and I followed.
Btw wee lady driving the Fiesta, sitting very close to the steering wheel, clearly nervous, clearly unused to city driving.

But anyway.
Not my circus, not my monkeys.

We went up the overpass on Station Street, over the bridge, down Anne Street and turned right onto Victoria Street.
I moved to the left lane to turn left into High Street.
He stayed in the lane to go straight ahead.

And then things went a bit wrong.
For him.

He decided he needed to be in my lane.
But I was in my lane.
And he didn't see me.
He started to move.

I could have slowed down.
I saw it happening.
I could have eased back.
I could have flashed the lights and let him in.
Quite easily.
I could have.
But I didn't.

I accelerated instead.
Then I blared the horn.
And my horn is louder than his horn.
And I held it longer than he held his.
And I gesticulated.
While blaring the horn.
And I yelled at him.
And he jerked back to the right.
And he refused to look at me.
Brave man with a wee woman in a wee Fiesta, not so brave with a big ugly bollox quite happy to blare back.
And he headed off down Victoria Street, staring straight ahead, hands at 10 to 2, into the distance for a wee diversion.

Sometimes an opportunity presents itself that makes it your circus, and makes them your monkeys.

Won't lie. It felt good. What a Dick.

12 May 2021, 16:11

We phoned Mollys Bar in Irvinestown and ordered two roast dinners yesterday.
Wee treat.
Great value too.
And a portion of chicken wings to start.
Just in case the dinners were small.
Better looking at it than looking for it.

I went to collect.
Nice wee lady.
In and paid.
Left a wee tip.
It's was Sunday. And she looked tired. And she was nice.
Out and waited.

She came out carrying two blue bags, straining at the weight. Arms hanging. Sweat glistening. Muscles heaving.
Order for Clampet she asked?
That's me says me.
And she opened the door and put both bags on the front seat.

The suspension groaned.
The tyres strained.
The seat creaked.

Are ye sure that's me says me?
I didn't order that much says me.
She looked at the docket.
2 roast dinners and chicken wings she says.
Yes says me.
Well then that's you she says.

I looked at the food up and down.

There's a big pile of food there says me.

She looked me up and down.
Well she says.
I told chef you were a big fella she says.
And you left us a tip she says.
So make sure not to leave ye hungry she says.
And she gave me a dirty wee seductive wink.

I love Fermanagh.

Where else would you be appraised, accommodated, admonished, and admired all the same time?

PS the dinners were lovely. Must phone and tell them.

17 May 2021, 15:16

Windy, glorious, powerful evening for a hike up Slieve Gullion.

We were on our way down.
I was in front, wee sister behind.
The wind picked up.
It was battering my face.
Whipping at my coat.
Tearing at my skin.
The temperature dropped.
I dropped my head.
I zipped up my coat.
I trudged on.

Are you OK I asked behind me?
Aye she replied.
The wind is biting says me.
Is it she says?
It's getting cold says me.
Really she says?

I stopped.
She stuck her head out from behind me.

Oh, so it is she said, surprised.
I couldn't feel it back here she said, giggling.
I was well sheltered she said, proudly.

And she gave me the dirtiest wee laugh and the sweetest big grin.

Aren't wee sisters deadly?? Anyone else and I would have huffed.

25 May 2021, 23:07

Morning all.

The reason you don't quite fit in is that you weren't born to fit in, you were born to stand out.

Average people fit it.
Exceptional people stand out.

Be different, be amazing, be wonderful, be creative, be kind, be intelligent, be exceptional, be loud, and be proud.

Have an exceptional day!!!

31 May 2021, 08:52

Printed in Great Britain
by Amazon